AF576968

The Bank Book

$ ¢ $ ¢ $

¢ $ ¢ $ ¢

$ ¢ $ ¢ ¢

¢ $ ¢ $ ¢

Naphtali Hoffman
and Stephen Brobeck

Edited by Jack Gillis

The Consumer Federation of America's Guide to the New Financial Marketplace

The Bank Book

How to Get the Most for Your Banking Dollars

A Harvest / HBJ Book

Harcourt Brace Jovanovich, Publishers

San Diego New York London

"Where to Find High-Yield CDs" reprinted by permission of
Savers Rate News, P.O. Box Drawer 52150, Miami, Florida 33152.

Library of Congress Cataloging in Publication Data

Hoffman, Naphtali.
The bank book.

"A Harvest/HBJ book."
Includes index.
1. Banks and banking—United States—Customer services.
2. Building and loan associations—United States.
3. Financial institutions—United States.
I. Brobeck, Stephen. II. Gillis, Jack.
III. Consumer Federation of America. IV. Title.
HG1616.C87H64 1986 332.1'7'0973 85-27271

ISBN 0-15-610676-0 (Harvest/HBJ : pbk.)

Designed by Michael Farmer
Printed in the United States of America
First Harvest/HBJ edition 1986
A B C D E F G H I J

To the good and dedicated people
who have led Cleveland Consumer Action

Contents

Preface

A revolution in financial services is transforming the way we pay for products, finance these purchases, and save money. We wrote *The Bank Book* principally to help consumers make sense of the radical changes and growing complexity in the new financial marketplace. The book explains as simply as possible all accounts and services offered by banking institutions. In addition, it includes specific information on accounts offered by hundreds of individual banks and savings and loans.

We prepared *The Bank Book* for two other purposes as well. The first was to enhance competition in consumer banking markets by disclosing information about the services of specific institutions. Banking products are so complex that many consumers will never fully understand them. To the extent this guide encourages banking institutions to offer more competitive services, however, all shoppers will benefit.

Our other goal was to demonstrate the need for additional consumer banking legislation. The most pressing need is for laws that require banking institutions to explain more clearly the terms of complex accounts. Our surveys and others have shown that these institutions could do a much better job of disclosing information about savings yields, conditions that limit these yields, fees and charges, check holds, and the terms of adjustable-rate mortgages. Laws similar to the Truth-in-Lending Act, passed by Congress in 1968, would serve this purpose well.

Both of us are deeply grateful to several colleagues for their assistance in the preparation of *The Bank Book.* Our greatest debt is to Susan Brobeck, who coordinated research on the accounts of more than 150 banks and savings and loans. She was ably assisted by Debra Hodes and Matt Mitchell. Banking experts Dr. Richard Morse, of Kansas State University, Ken McEldowney, of San Francisco Consumer Action, Alan Fox, of Consumer Federation of America, Mary Reardon, of the Credit Union National Association, former bank trust officer Carol Hoffman, Brenda Schneider, of Manufacturers National Bank in Detroit, William McKenzie, of Elmira Savings and Loan, Meredith Fernstrom and Peggy Haney, of American Express, and Jim Callan, of the Electronic Funds Transfer Association offered invaluable criticism of our manuscript, while Lisa Goldstein and William Smith assisted greatly in its preparation. Finally, we wish to thank Dr. John Brobeck, Jack Gillis, and Harcourt Brace Jovanovich editor Martha Lawrence for immeasurably improving the accuracy and clarity of the text.

S.B. & N.H.

Introduction

This is the book for every consumer who has recently paid $20 for a "bounced" check, waited two weeks for access to deposited funds, established a money market fund for an interest rate that lasted only three months, or tried to figure out the difference between a money market deposit account and a money market fund. This book is for every American facing the new, complex, and increasingly expensive world of personal finance.

The corner bank is going the way of the corner drugstore. No longer can you, or should you, depend on one institution to meet all your financial needs. But who should you turn to? What type of checking account or savings account should you have? How can you decide where to open it? What rights do you have in the financial marketplace? How is new technology changing the control you have over your personal finances?

The Bank Book answers these questions and many more. This book provides you with a clear, simple method of using and benefiting from the wide array of new banking services. It also helps you avoid the pitfalls, explains your rights, and provides you with actual cost comparisons based on a nationwide survey of major financial institutions in the United States. In short, *The Bank Book* is a definitive, comparative guide that will tell you how to choose the best services from among today's banking products.

The deregulation of the banking industry has caused a revolution in the financial marketplace. There are hundreds of new products, and prices for once free services have skyrocketed. In 1983, banks collected $10 billion in service charges on all deposit accounts—an amount that had doubled in four years.

Banking institutions have introduced so many competing services that selecting the best from among them has become difficult, if not impossible. While offering more options and higher interest, this new competition has introduced considerable consumer confusion.

Choosing from among financial services and accounts has become so frustrating for many that Congress and other government agencies have been flooded with complaints about the proliferation of fees, reduced services, extended check holding times, and the general lack of customer concern displayed by many banks and other financial institutions. The result is growing consumer unrest and dissatisfaction.

Specific conditions stimulating the need for help include:

- The dramatic increase in new accounts, including IRAs, money market deposit accounts, NOW accounts, and SuperNOW accounts, all unheard of a few years ago.
- The introduction of variable rates on loans and deposits, including adjustable-rate mortgages, installment loans, certificates of deposit, and money market funds.
- New and increased charges for every category of service, including phone calls to learn balances, credit card fees, and low-balance penalties on savings accounts.
- More banking by machines (ATMs), by phone (telephone bill-payer), and by computer (home banking).

Responding to the growing evidence of consumer concern, the rise in consumer complaints, and the failure of many institutions to respond satisfactorily, the Consumer Federation of America has prepared this comprehensive, comparative guide to banking services. The book names names among the nation's largest financial institutions, exposing the best instruments and services as well as the rip-offs. It will give the average consumer the same marketplace advantage enjoyed by major investors.

The Bank Book covers all consumer banking services as well as nonbank options such as money market funds and mutual funds. Special features include:

- Summary recommendations at the beginning of almost every chapter.
- Easy-to-use checklists to facilitate cost comparisons.
- Simple explanations of all types of accounts, including when to use them and how to choose them.
- Specific information on consumer accounts at more than 150 of the nation's largest financial institutions in the sixteen largest metropolitan markets.

This information was gathered by Consumer Federation of America in late 1984 and 1985. It was supplemented by data on interest rates collected by other agencies in late 1985. Even though much of the specific information in *The Bank Book* is accurate today, banking institutions change the terms of their accounts often enough that you should not assume this information has remained unchanged. Before purchasing a specific banking product, check its current price, yield, and other features yourself.

The Bank Book

1

Checking and NOW Accounts

RECOMMENDATIONS

The best checking accounts for those who can meet balance requirements are NOW accounts or credit union share drafts. Select the one with the lowest minimum (or average) balance that allows you to earn interest and avoid fees. Do not hold surplus funds in a checking account. Invest the funds in a savings account paying a higher interest rate.

If you cannot meet the NOW account minimum, select a regular checking account with the lowest minimum balance to avoid charges. (These minimums are usually lower than NOW account minimums.) If you cannot maintain this checking minimum, look for a "lifeline" account.

When selecting a checking account, shopping around pays off. In fact, most consumers can save more than $100 per year by comparing monthly service and transaction fees. Fees tend to be lower at savings and loans (S & Ls) than at banks.

continued on next page

continued

As you compare costs, look for an institution that has short holding periods on deposited checks and that will contact you before bouncing a check. Ask for a credit line; it can save you the expense and hassle of bounced checks.

The Revolution in Checking

With the exception of payment by cash, writing checks is the most frequent way consumers transfer funds. Seventy-nine percent maintain some type of checking account, and the typical household writes about twenty-four checks per month. A large majority of these accounts are with full-service banking institutions—commercial banks, S & Ls, or credit unions.

In the 1980s, checking accounts changed in several important respects. First, in 1980 the federal government permitted credit unions to issue interest-bearing share drafts, and in early 1981 it allowed banks and savings and loans to pay interest on the money in checking accounts. These accounts are called "Negotiable Order of Withdrawal" or "NOW" accounts.

Second, partly to make up the interest paid to customers on NOW accounts, banking institutions substantially increased their fees for writing, depositing, bouncing, and stopping payment on checks. Between 1979 and 1983, total fees charged by banks on all checking and savings accounts rose from $5 to 10 billion. Today, these fees continue to grow. Our survey revealed that banks are now charging monthly service fees as high as $15 for regular checking and $25 for a NOW account. Moreover, some charge as much as .50 to write a check, $1.00 to make a deposit, .60 to use an automatic teller machine, $30 for a bounced check, and $20 to stop payment on a check.

Third, banking institutions now offer a variety of new services related to checking. These include direct deposit, bill-payer services, and telephone transfer. Each of these new services has increased the convenience of banking.

Checking Options

There are five basic types of checking accounts; three of these earn interest (NOW, SuperNOW, and share drafts) and two do not. The two types of non-interest-earning accounts are called "no-minimum" and "regular" checking. Most banks offer all types of accounts but share drafts. S & Ls offer only NOW and SuperNOW accounts. Credit unions issue share drafts. The following table summarizes the *typical* features of these five accounts.

Table 1
CHECKING ACCOUNTS: TYPICAL FEATURES

Type of Account	*Minimum to Earn Interest*	*Interest Rate (%)*	*Minimum to Avoid Fees*	*Monthly Service Charge*	*Per-Check Charge*
No-Minimum	NA	NA	NA	$3.00	$.25
Regular Checking	NA	NA	$ 500	3.00	.25
NOW	$ 100	5.25%	1000	5.00	.25
SuperNOW	2500	7.5	2500	5.00	.25
Share Draft	237	5.9	300	3.00	.15

If you cannot keep the minimum balance of a regular account, you will find that the charges for no-minimum checking are less *if you write few checks*. But if you can maintain the minimum, it is better to have a regular account, since no fees will be assessed.

Most NOW accounts have two minimum (or average) balance requirements: a minimum required to earn interest and a higher minimum to avoid fees. The minimum to avoid fees is usually higher than on regular checking, too, but much lower than the $2500 minimum on most SuperNOW accounts.

Although the fees in the table above are typical, they are not the same at all institutions. In fact, we found the monthly minimum to avoid fees on regular checking to be much higher than the no-fee minimum on certain NOW accounts. In some cases, the monthly fee on regular checking was higher than the fee charged on NOW and SuperNOW accounts. On average, S & Ls charged lower fees than did banks. Also, roughly half of banking institutions offer free checking to seniors.

No-Minimum Checking

No-minimum checking is offered by fewer than half of all banks. These accounts are advertised for infrequent check writers with low balances. No interest is paid on these accounts. The fees are often advertised as lower than those on regular checking and NOW accounts. Our survey found, however, that no-minimum fees are not significantly lower than those on regular checking except on lifeline accounts. Lifeline accounts typically charge no or very low fees, but limit the number of transactions, most commonly to between five and ten monthly. They are offered by only a few institutions, which sometimes tie them to automated teller machine (ATM) use.

■ Fees.

Monthly service or transaction fees are charged on most no-minimum accounts. Typically, there is a monthly service fee and/or charge for each check written. When only one or the other fee is charged, the fees are higher. For example, a typical fee is $3 a month for service and .25 for each check written. If there is only a monthly fee, it is likely to be $5; if there is only a per-check charge, it is likely to be .30 to .35. Some institutions also charge fees for deposits (individual checks and/or deposit slips) and ATM transactions.

Our survey uncovered monthly service fees ranging from nothing to $6 at Bay Bank, Boston. Most often, they were $2.25 to $3.50. Per-check charges ranged from nothing to .50 at Bank of America, with most .20 or .25. Most institutions did not charge a fee for making a deposit, but when they did, it was usually .25 per check.

■ Cost to Consumers.

The cost of maintaining a no-minimum checking account varies with both the institution and the level of activity. The following table outlines the actual cost of a no-minimum account at various banks across the country.

Table 2 reveals that the cost of identical accounts varies considerably from bank to bank. The cost for infrequent check writers (five per month) can vary from $15 to $68, and for frequent check writers (thirty per month) it can vary threefold ($60 to $197). These differences demonstrate the importance of shopping around. Unless you are an infrequent check writer at an institution with low fees, no-minimum checking is expensive compared to other options.

Regular Checking

Regular checking is usually offered only by banks. Unlike no-minimum accounts, monthly service and transaction fees are not assessed when a minimum (or average) balance is maintained. When this balance is not kept, nearly all banks charge a monthly service fee and most assess per-check fees as well.

■ Minimums to Avoid Fees.

The minimum balance required to avoid charges on a regular checking account varies greatly, ranging from a low of $100 to a high of $2500. For most accounts in our survey, the minimum balance was $500.

Table 2
NO-MINIMUM CHECKING ACCOUNTS: HOW MUCH DO THEY COST?

Institution	*Monthly Charges*				*Annual Cost* Number of Checks per Month*			
	Service Charge	*Check Charge*	*Deposit Charge*	*ATM Charge*	*5*	*10*	*20*	*30*
Union Trust Baltimore	$2.25	$.35		$.25	$60	$81	$123	$165
Bank of Boston Boston	3.00	.25	$.40	.15	68	83	113	143
Harris Chicago	3.00	.20			48	60	84	108
Ameritrust Cleveland	1.50	.25			33	48	78	108
First Texas Dallas		.25			15	30	60	90
Manufacturers Detroit	3.00	.30			54	72	108	144
Riggs D.C.	3.00	.20			48	60	84	108
Security Pacific Los Angeles	3.50	.25			57	72	102	132

National Westminster								
New York	3.25	.30			57	75	111	147
Central								
Pittsburgh		.35		.25	33	54	96	138
Mark Twain								
St. Louis	1.00	.20			24	36	60	84
Bank of America								
San Francisco								
Account #1	5.00				60	60	60	60
Account #2		.50		.35	47	77	137	197
Average cost					$45	$69	$ 91	$119

* Also includes 2 deposits and 4 ATM transactions per month

Table 3
MINIMUM BALANCE TO AVOID FEES ON REGULAR CHECKING

Minimum Balance	*Percentage of Institutions (%)*
$1500 and above	5
1000–1999	5
700–999	10
600–699	10
500–599	48
300–499	19
100–299	3
	100

Most banks provide consumers the option of maintaining an average balance, which is usually higher than the minimum. If your checking balance fluctuates greatly, this option can save you money. There is a tremendous range ($100 to $5000) in the amount required for an average-balance account. Typically, the average balance is $1000.

Table 4
AVERAGE BALANCE TO AVOID FEES ON REGULAR CHECKING

Average Balance	*Percentage of Institutions (%)*
$2500 and above	3
1500–2499	21
1000–1499	59
700–999	7
500–699	7
100–499	3
	100

■ Fees.

When minimum or average balances are not maintained, fees are assessed. Almost all banks charge a monthly service fee that may vary depending on the balance—the lower the balance, the higher the fee. Most also charge a fee for each check written. Monthly service fees at these banks are usually lower than those at institutions without per-check charges. A number of institutions with per-check fees also charge for deposits and/or for ATM transactions.

Banks in the same area tend to charge the same types of fees, but the amounts often differ. In Chicago, Dallas, and St. Louis, for example, banks charge fairly high monthly service fees but no transaction charges. On the other hand, banks in Boston, Detroit, Los Angeles, and San Francisco tend to assess both lower monthly fees and per-check charges.

Our survey showed a huge range in monthly service fees—from $1.50 at First Seneca in Pittsburgh to $15 at Bankers Trust in New York City. Whereas the most frequent fee is $3, more than one-quarter of the banks charged at least $6.

Per-check charges ranged from nothing to .50 at Manufacturers Hanover in New York. The most common fee is .25. Fees for making a deposit vary from nothing at most banks to .50, again at Manufacturers Hanover. When charged, the most typical deposit fee is .25. ATM transaction charges range from nothing at most banks to .25 at First National Bank in Minneapolis.

Table 5
MONTHLY SERVICE FEES ON REGULAR CHECKING

Fees	*Percentage of Institutions (%)*
$10–20	10
7–9.99	11
6–6.99	6
5–5.99	13
4–4.99	13
3–3.99	27
2–2.99	18
1–1.99	2
	100

■ Cost to Consumers.

The annual cost of maintaining a regular checking account when the minimum balance requirement is not met varies considerably—from \$36 to \$90 for infrequent check writers, and from \$36 to \$165 for frequent check writers. Particularly for moderate and frequent check writers, it is important to maintain the minimum or average balance necessary to avoid these fees. If this is impossible, moderate and frequent check writers should select an account with a monthly service charge but no transaction fees.

NOW Accounts

NOW accounts are offered by almost all banks and S & Ls. When minimum (or average) balances are kept, the interest earned is almost always 5¼%. When somewhat higher minimum or average balances are maintained, there are usually no monthly service and transaction fees. NOW account minimums (and averages) are usually higher than those on regular checking. When the minimums are not met, the fees are also generally higher.

■ Interest Minimums and Rates.

Our survey found that at most banks and S & Ls either no minimum balance must be maintained to earn interest or the minimum is fairly low (under \$200). There were some notable exceptions. For example, at Home Savings in Los Angeles, the minimum was \$2000; at Huntington in Cleveland and National Westminster in New York, it was \$1500; and at Bankers Trust in New York, an average balance of \$5000 had to be kept to earn interest.

Nearly all institutions pay the maximum allowable rate of 5¼%, but it is often compounded in different ways. About one-fifth do so continuously, one-fifth monthly, and the remainder daily. The most favorable method to consumers is continuous compounding on a

Table 6
ANNUAL COST OF REGULAR CHECKING ACCOUNT WHEN MINIMUM BALANCE NOT MAINTAINED

Institution	*Monthly Charges*				*Annual Cost* Number of Checks per Month*			
	Service Charge	*Check Charge*	*Deposit Charge*	*ATM Charge*	*5*	*10*	*20*	*30*
Union Trust Baltimore	$2.25	$.35		$.25	$60	$81	$123	$165
Bank of Boston Boston	3.00	.30	$.30	.15	68	86	122	158
Harris Chicago	5.00				60	60	60	60
Ameritrust Cleveland	3.00	.18			47	58	79	101
First Texas Dallas	4.00				48	48	48	48
Manufacturers Detroit	3.00	.30			54	72	108	144
Riggs D.C.	7.50†				90	90	90	90
Security Pacific Los Angeles	3.50	.25			57	72	102	132

Table 6 continued
ANNUAL COST OF REGULAR CHECKING ACCOUNT WHEN MINIMUM BALANCE NOT MAINTAINED

Institution	*Monthly Charges*				*Annual Cost* Number of Checks per Month*			
	Service Charge	*Check Charge*	*Deposit Charge*	*ATM Charge*	*5*	*10*	*20*	*30*
National Westminster								
New York	7.00†				84	84	84	84
Central								
Pittsburgh	3.00‡	.20			48	60	84	108
Mark Twain								
St. Louis	3.00‡				36	36	36	36
Bank of America								
San Francisco	3.00	.30			54	72	108	144

* Also includes 2 deposits and 4 ATM transactions per month
† Under $500 minimum balance
‡ Under $300 minimum balance

365/360-day basis. But unless huge balances are involved, the difference between continuous and daily compounding is not significant—less than one-tenth of 1% in interest earned.

■ Minimums to Avoid Fees.

At almost all banks and S & Ls, minimum (or average) balances must be maintained to avoid monthly service and transaction fees. The minimum in our survey ranged from $100 to $5000. Most institutions had a minimum between $500 and $1500, with $1000 most common.

Table 7
MINIMUM BALANCE TO AVOID FEES ON NOW ACCOUNTS

Minimum Balance	*Percentage of Institutions (%)*
$5000	2
2500–4999	8
2000–2499	8
1500–1999	11
1000–1499	39
500–999	24
0–499	8
	100

To allow you to avoid regular fees, some institutions offer the option of keeping an average balance in a NOW account *or* a minimum balance in a savings account. These average balances can range from $1000 to $5000, with most between $2000 and $3000. For banks that offered the savings-account/minimum-balance option in our survey, the minimums ranged from $1000 to $10,000.

■ Fees.

When minimum balances are not maintained, monthly service and/or transaction fees are charged. At most institutions these fees are either the same as or somewhat higher than similar fees on regular checking; they are never lower. Also, monthly service fees tend to be highest at those banks and S & Ls without transaction charges.

Again, our survey showed a wide range in monthly service fees, from $3 to $20. The most common charge was $5.

Table 8
MONTHLY SERVICE FEES ON NOW ACCOUNTS

Monthly Fees	*Percentage of Institutions*
$10–20.00	15
7–9.99	14
6–6.99	11
5–5.99	30
4–4.99	11
3–3.99	19
2–2.99	0
	100

About half of all institutions surveyed charged a fee for each NOW check written. This check charge was usually in addition to monthly service fees. The charge to write a check ranged from .10 to .50 at Manufacturers Hanover (which also charged a $10 monthly service fee). The typical fee was .25. A few banks and S & Ls also charged a fee for deposits. When charged, this fee ranged from .12 to .50 at Manufacturers Hanover. The most common fee was .30. In addition, a small but growing number of institutions are charging for ATM transactions. These fees varied from .15 to .60 for a withdrawal at D.C. National Bank. The typical charge was .15.

■ Cost to Consumers.

The annual cost of maintaining a NOW account when minimum balance requirements are not met ranges from $53 to $144 for very infrequent check writers, and from $72 to $198 for frequent check writers, as shown in Table 9.

The considerable rise in costs for frequent check writers is illustrated by the Bank of Boston, where the cost rises from $68 to

$158. This emphasizes the importance, to frequent check writers, of maintaining minimum or average balance requirements. If this is not possible, choose a regular checking account with a low monthly service fee and no transaction charges.

SuperNOW Accounts

SuperNOW accounts are NOW accounts that pay a higher interest rate if a higher minimum balance is maintained. Federal law permits this minimum to be as low as $1000, but most banks require $2500. Unlike NOW accounts, where the 5¼% interest is fixed by law, SuperNOW accounts have a variable interest rate. Most recently the typical rate was just under 7%.

At many institutions SuperNOW accounts are automatically treated as NOW accounts during those months when the minimum is not reached. These combination accounts offer the advantages of convenience and lower cost. It is easier to open and maintain one, rather than two, accounts. And if the balance dips below the SuperNOW minimum, interest is still earned and transaction fees are not assessed as long as the NOW account minimum is maintained.

Nevertheless, keeping large sums of money in SuperNOW accounts is not recommended. You can earn more interest by investing these savings in some other vehicle—a certificate of deposit, a money market account, or a non-bank savings option. Money market accounts, for example, currently pay an interest rate that is somewhat higher than the SuperNOW rate.

Share Drafts

Interest-bearing checking accounts called "share drafts" are offered by about 30% of all credit unions. They are the credit union equivalent of regular NOW accounts offered by banks and S & Ls.

Most credit unions offering these accounts impose no routine charges, regardless of the size of the account. Among the few that

Table 9
COST OF A NOW ACCOUNT WHEN MINIMUMS NOT MAINTAINED

Institution	*Monthly Charges*				*Annual Cost* Number of Checks per Month*			
	Service Charge	*Check Charge*	*Deposit Charge*	*ATM Charge*	*5*	*10*	*20*	*30*
Union Trust Baltimore	$ 2.25	$.35		$.25	$ 60	$ 81	$123	$165
Bank of Boston Boston	3.00	.30	$.30	.15	68	86	122	158
Harris Chicago	6.00				72	72	72	72
Ameritrust Cleveland	4.00	.25			63	78	108	138
First Texas Dallas	7.50				90	90	90	90
Manufacturers Detroit	7.50	.30			108	126	162	198
Riggs D.C.	12.00				144	144	144	144
Security Pacific Los Angeles	5.00	.20	.20		77	89	113	137

National Westminster								
New York	7.00				84	84	84	84
Central								
Pittsburgh	3.00	.20		.10	53	65	89	113
Mark Twain								
St. Louis	6.00				72	72	72	72
Bank of America								
San Francisco	4.00	.30		.15	73	91	127	163

* Also includes 2 deposits and 4 ATM transactions per month

do charge, fees can often be avoided by keeping a minimum balance in the account, which is relatively low—$300 on average. Credit unions that charge when the account is below the minimum impose average fees of $3.00 per month.

Few credit unions charge a fee for each check written, and less than 2% offering share drafts impose both monthly and per-check fees. The average per-check fee at credit unions is .15.

Most credit unions require no minimum balance to earn interest on checking accounts, and among those that do, the balance is small, averaging $237. The average interest rate paid on checking accounts in credit unions is 5.9%.

Special Charges and Limits

■ Check Purchases.

Most banks and S & Ls offer several types of checks. The cost depends on whether the checks are personalized or printed on fancy paper. The price of checks varies little from institution to institution. For instance, the cost of purchasing two hundred of the least expensive checks varied only from $5 to $8.50 in our survey. Thus, this expense should not be a major factor in choosing an account.

■ Check Holds.

Banks and S & Ls "hold" some deposited checks for a period of time before releasing the funds to you. These holding periods typically rise as the distance increases between the bank on which the check was written and the bank where the check was deposited. The longest holding periods are usually on checks from distant regions of the country.

Check holds range widely—from no delay to as many as thirty days on out-of-state checks. These periods are the shortest in states that have set limits by law. New York, for example, requires commercial banks to clear in-town checks in one business day, in-state checks in two, and out-of-state checks in five.

Lengthy check holds irritate millions of consumers who, thinking funds are available, write checks that then bounce. Not only are many of these consumers charged for the overdrafts, but they are also forced to spend time straightening out the mess. You can avoid this irritation by selecting an institution with short holding periods, or one that is willing to arrange the immediate release of deposited funds. Some banks will agree not to hold pay checks or deposited checks if an equivalent amount is maintained in a savings account.

Most credit unions do not have policies on holding checks. Those that do typically hold local checks for three to five days and out-of-state checks for seven to ten days.

■ Overdrafts.

The price of bouncing a check ranged from $6 at Citibank, the Bank of California, and California First to $30 at Mellon in Philadelphia. There is no typical charge for overdrafts. At credit unions the charge for bounced checks averaged $9.24.

Table 10
COST OF BOUNCED CHECKS AT BANKS AND S & Ls

Charges	*Percentage of Institutions (%)*
$20–30	18
17–19	4
14–16	25
11–13	13
9–10	27
7–8	9
6 or less	4
	100

■ Stop Payments.

The cost of stopping payment on a check varies considerably—from $4 at California First to $20 at Texas American in Dallas and First American in D.C. But as Table 11 indicates, these charges are generally less than those for overdrafts.

Table 11
COST OF STOP PAYMENTS AT BANKS AND S & Ls

Charges	*Percentage of Institutions (%)*
$20	3
17–19	3
14–16	10
11–13	13
9–10	26
7–8	17
6 or less	28
	100

■ Canceled Check Truncation.

Most consumers value receiving canceled checks. These provide a far more complete and valuable record of payments than do monthly statements.

Yet banking institutions have been trying to truncate this service—that is, retain the canceled checks themselves and provide consumers with only a monthly statement listing check numbers and amounts. Truncation allows banks to avoid the time and expense of mailing canceled checks to consumers.

To encourage consumer acceptance of truncation, banks have resorted to several strategies. A few simply impose it, allowing no other option. But most offer incentives to encourage truncation, such as lower fees or the payment of interest.

Institutions with truncated accounts will make available copies of checks, but usually for a fee. This charge ranges from nothing to $5. Two dollars or $3 is a typical fee.

■ Inquiries.

Increasingly, banks and S & Ls charge fees for providing information about personal accounts. A growing number now charge a fee for responding to a phone inquiry about your checking balance. About half the institutions in our sample still did not charge for this service, but one-third did, usually for a fee of $1 or $2. (The remaining institutions do not provide information on account balances over the phone.)

■ Inactive Accounts and Early Closure.

Some banks and S & Ls charge consumers for accounts that are inactive or closed within a year of opening. One bank, for example, charges a monthly fee of $2 on accounts under $500 with no transactions in the previous six months. It continues to assess the fee until a check is written, a deposit is made, or the customer notifies the bank that he or she is aware the account exists.

Less reasonable is the practice of charging a fee for closing an account within a year after it is opened. Marine Midland in New York, for instance, charges $25 for terminating an account within the first year. Since you may wish to close an account early if your bank substantially hikes its charges, you should avoid banks that charge closure fees.

Special Services

■ Credit Lines.

Many banks and S & Ls offer a credit line that becomes an automatic loan if you write a check for more than your account balance

These loan programs are variously called "credit lines," "no–bounce checking," "overdraft privileges," "cash advance," and "advance" accounts. They are similar in that they lend you funds to cover overdrafts. A credit line can help you avoid bounced-check fees.

Institutions lend either the exact amount of the overdraft or an amount in a multiple of $500 or $100. The total advanced can range from $300 to $7500. The annual percentage rates (APR) charged on these loans approximate those charged on unpaid credit purchases—roughly 18% to 22%. In addition, some institutions assess a monthly service fee or a per-loan fee when overdrafts are covered.

The method of repayment varies considerably. Some institutions automatically repay the loan or loans with deposited funds, either the day of the deposit or at the end of the billing period. Other institutions require you to make formal payment, usually after receiving monthly statements. Many make a predetermined automatic payment from funds in the account on the statement date.

Generally, the smaller the credit line, the easier it is to obtain. Some institutions require you to fill out an extensive credit application; others will extend this protection to you if you are a long-term customer who has demonstrated an ability to manage your account. At some institutions a credit line is a feature of the bank card and available only to customers who have a card.

■ Bill-Payer Services.

A number of banks and S & Ls are willing to to make designated payments for their checking customers. Perpetual American in D.C., for example, allows customers to authorize individual payments by phone on regular monthly payments of rent, electricity bills, mortgage payments, and other continuing obligations. The charge for this service is often less than the cost of postage, and it offers such great convenience that you should consider selecting a bank or S & L with this feature if the cost is reasonable. The only risk is the increased difficulty in resolving disputes about bills. Once the bank makes a payment it may be harder to persuade a utility or other payee that a bill in dispute should be adjusted.

■ Telephone Transfer.

A few banks allow customers to transfer funds by phone between checking and savings accounts. This service can be useful in helping you keep sufficient funds in a checking account to avoid overdrafts or monthly service or transaction fees.

Miscellaneous Services

■ Safe-Deposit Boxes.

These boxes are useful for keeping jewelry and valuable papers, including securities, insurance policies, and proof of insured valuables. Unfortunately, the price of renting safe-deposit boxes has risen significantly. In our survey, the annual rental averaged $15, up from under $10 several years ago. The highest yearly fee was $40, at the Bank of Boston. Yet, there are banking institutions that rent to depositors for an annual fee under $10. And some institutions will waive the fee entirely if substantial deposits, ranging in our survey from $2500 to $7500, are maintained.

■ Money Orders and Cashier's Checks.

Consumers without a checking account may wish to pay bills and make other funds transfers with money orders. Ten years ago, most of these payments cost less than .50. Today, according to our survey, most money orders cost between $1 and $1.50, and ranged as high as $10. At $1.50 each, writing five money orders a month would cost $90 a year. This expense is considerably more than that of writing checks on an account in which the minimum balance to avoid fees is maintained.

Some banking institutions sell money orders only to depositors. Others assess regular customers a lower fee. Dallas Federal, for example, charges depositors $2 and nondepositors $4.

Banks and S & Ls sell cashier's checks as an alternative to money orders. Although both serve the same purpose, institutions limit the size of money orders, but not the size of cashier's checks. Typically, they charge the same price for a money order and a cashier's check of the same amount. But they assess a high fee for cashier's checks written for large amounts.

■ Check Cashing.

Most banks and S & Ls in our survey cashed only the third-party checks of depositors. They did not even cash the Social Security and welfare checks of noncustomers. Institutions that are willing to do so typically assess high fees—as high as $7 per check. But Ameritrust in Cleveland is a notable exception. For more than a year, its branches have cashed the government checks of nondepositors for free.

CHECKLIST

Use this checklist when shopping for checking or NOW accounts.

Only NOW Accounts

Interest rate ____________

Method of compounding ____________

Minimum (average) balance to earn interest ____________

NOW and Checking Accounts

Minimum balance to avoid regular fee ____________

Regular fees

- Monthly service ____________
- Per check written ____________
- Per deposit ____________
- Per ATM transfer ____________

Special fees

- Bounced check ____________
- Stop payment ____________
- Returned deposits ____________
- Purchasing checks ____________
- Balance inquiries ____________
- Early closure ____________

Other features

- Check holds (in town, in state, out of state) ____________
- Interest paid during hold period ____________
- Required truncation ____________
- Bill-payer services and cost ____________
- Telephone transfer ____________
- Credit line, amount and cost ____________

$ ¢ $ ¢ $

¢ $ ¢ $ ¢

$ ¢ $ ¢ $

¢ $ ¢ $ ¢

2

Electronic Funds Transfers

The implementation of new electronic technologies has made it possible for banks to offer you new ways to obtain cash, deposit pay checks, pay for purchases, transfer funds between accounts, obtain information about accounts, and secure other services. These activities are called "electronic funds transfers" (EFTs). Currently available to a number of consumers are automated teller machines (ATMs), debit cards, telephone bill-payer, home banking, and direct deposit.

Automated Teller Machines (ATMs)

ATMs, available at many banks, S & Ls, and some credit unions, perform services previously available only from tellers. They can be used by customers who have obtained a plastic ATM card and a personal identification number (PIN) or name (PIC). At the end of 1984, nearly fifty thousand of these machines were in operation and being used by about one-third of all bank customers.

■ Services.

By far the most popular service offered by ATMs is the disbursement of cash. ATMs usually dispense cash in $5, $20 or $25 multiples up to $200 or $300. Larger amounts are available only from tellers.

ATMs perform other services as well. Although these vary from bank to bank, they often include providing information on account balances, accepting check and cash deposits, transferring funds between accounts, and even paying bills.

Increasingly, the ATM networks of different institutions are being linked together so that you can obtain services at other banks or at supermarkets, convenience stores, shopping centers, office buildings, and airports. Today, most of the more than 250 networks are local or regional, but in the future they will be combined to link regions and cities throughout the nation.

■ How to Shop for ATMs.

ATMs offer you greatly increased convenience. In most cases, you can obtain cash far more quickly than from tellers, and at any hour of the day or night. However, ATMs differ from institution to institution, so it is important to shop around. Pay particular attention to seven factors:

1. Does the ATM network offer the specific services you desire? If you would like it to transfer funds between your checking and savings accounts, will it do so?

2. Are machines available in convenient locations? Are they easily accessible to home and workplace? Does the network serve places you may travel to in your area or outside it?

3. Are the ATMs easy to use? Are the instructions simple and clear? Can you read the screens? Insist that you see a demonstration of one of the bank's machines before you apply for their ATM card.

4. Can the ATMs be used in privacy? It is especially important that no one can read your identification number or name as you punch it in. With this PIN or PIC and your card, a thief can easily

steal funds from your accounts until you report the loss of your card.

5. Does the ATM take a photo of each transaction? This photo provides a record of all transactions and can be especially useful in the event your card is used by someone without your permission or the bank claims to have no record of a deposit. Unfortunately, only a relatively small number of ATMs offer this feature.

6. Are the machines located in well-lighted, glass-enclosed vestibules accessible only to those with bank cards? ATM location and placement are particularly important to those who need to use them at night or in high-crime areas.

7. Does the bank assess transaction charges for using ATMs? A small but growing number of banks charge you for cash withdrawals and other transactions at bank ATMs. In our survey, charges ranged from .15 to .45 per transaction, but at one institution they were $1.00. Even a .25 charge assessed twice a week can cost you $26 annually. There is almost always a transaction charge for using network ATMs at non-bank locations like supermarkets.

■ How to Use ATMs.

Since ATMs are riskier to use than tellers, you should follow these seven rules:

1. Do not write your identification code number or name on your ATM card or on any paper you carry in your wallet or purse. Although this may seem obvious, a surprisingly large number of consumers unthinkingly record their PIN or PIC in a place accessible to a thief. Instead, memorize the code.

2. Do not use an ATM if there is significant risk of theft. For example, do not withdraw cash at night from an exposed, poorly lighted machine located in a high-crime area.

3. When using an ATM, make certain to conceal your PIN or PIC as you enter it. Sometimes thieves pretend they are ATM customers to try to see your identification code, then pick your pocket to obtain your ATM card.

4. Do not make cash deposits. There is no verifiable record of this deposit—only the receipt you have created—so you run the risk of losing your deposit if the bank makes an error or a bank employee steals your cash. The risk of depositing checks is much less, since cashed checks remain as a record.

5. When you make a deposit or withdrawal, make certain you get a receipt and check its accuracy. Institutions operating ATMs are required to provide you with this record. Make certain to complain if you do not receive one, or if it is inaccurate.

6. Compare these receipts with your monthly statements to check for potentially costly bank errors. Call any discrepancies to the attention of the bank.

7. If your ATM card is lost or stolen, immediately inform the bank. If this loss or any unauthorized transaction is reported within two days, you are liable only for losses up to $50. After two days your liability increases to $500.

Debit Cards

Debit cards are a new method of paying for purchases. These plastic cards allow merchants to deduct the price of purchases immediately from your bank account. If your account contains insufficient funds, you cannot make the purchase.

Most of the several million debit cards outstanding have been issued by banks. Several major oil companies now offer debit cards that can be used at their own service stations and sometimes at the stations of other companies. In the future, department stores and other retailers may also issue their own debit cards.

Banks and others promoting these cards hope they will increasingly replace checks. Because the electronic funds transfers permitted by debit cards can be much less costly than more labor-intensive check processing, banks are trying to persuade retailers to install point-of-sale (POS) equipment. By the beginning of 1985, banks had convinced five thousand retailers to install some eight thousand POS terminals.

Presently, debit cards offer few advantages compared to other payment methods. They are most useful to those who make payments out of town but don't want to use credit cards.

■ Advantages.

Debit cards do have some advantages over payment by personal check. They are easier to carry, more readily accepted out of town by establishments with POS equipment, and cost little or nothing to use. Currently, few banks impose a monthly fee or assess transaction charges for debit cards. Compared to truncated checking accounts, debit cards supply a fuller record of transactions: monthly statements include the payee; checking statements do not.

Compared to credit card payment, the only two advantages of payment by debit card are that fees are lower and impulse buying is discouraged. Debit cards do not permit you to spend funds that are not in your bank account.

■ Disadvantages.

In contrast to payment by check and especially by credit card, debit cards have several major drawbacks.

First, you run the risk of embarrassment from being told at the cash register that you have insufficient funds to make a purchase. When ATMs are installed in stores so that you can check your bank balance prior to a purchase, this will cease to be a problem. But ATMs are currently available at few retail outlets.

Second, you lose the lengthy float of most credit cards and the short float of most checks. In fully functioning POS systems, funds are immediately deducted from your account. You do not have the thirty grace days available on most credit card purchases.

Third, it is more difficult to resolve disputes over purchases made with debit cards. If goods are not delivered, or if they are of unsatisfactory quality, you can stop payment on a check or refuse to make the related credit card payment. Since funds are immediately deducted on a debit card purchase, you have much less leverage in dealing with retailers who treat you unfairly.

Fourth, you are exposed to greater liability if your debit card is lost or stolen than if your credit card is taken. Unless you notify the bank within two days, you may be liable for unauthorized use up to $500. This liability is only $50 on credit cards.

■ The Future.

In coming years, many banks and retailers will aggressively market debit cards as an alternative to checks. To the extent that they are much cheaper to use than checks, these cards will become more attractive. Yet debit cards will not be used by many as an alternative to credit cards unless banks eliminate the float period on the later. If they do, many credit card users who pay off balances fully are likely to shift to debit cards, provided the latter remain less expensive to use.

Telephone Bill-Payer

More than three hundred banking institutions offer telephone bill-payer services that permit you to pay bills by phone. If you opt for this service, you must first complete an authorization form and list of payees. The offering institution will then send you a verification statement, numerical codes for your payees, an account number, and a numerical secret code. To pay bills, you must call the bill-payer phone number, dial the account number and secret code, then enter each payee code and payment amount.

Bill-payer services usually can be used twenty-four hours a day, seven days a week. Some even offer a toll-free 800 number so that you can make payments from out of town. Most services also include a number that can be called for assistance.

To use such a service, you must have access to a push-button phone. If you have the old rotary-type telephone, your message must be given by voice to an operator, who activates the system.

Costs vary from service to service, yet often include the same types of charges as the account from which funds are drawn to make payments. At a typical institution in our survey, bill-payer funds drawn from a NOW account required a $2 monthly fee if the minimum monthly balance dipped below $1000 but remained above $500, and a $4 monthly fee if the balance fell below $500.

Home Banking

The purchase of a personal computer has permitted many families to do much of their banking at home. With a modem and phone, you link your computer to one at the bank so the two can "converse" through telephone lines. Once you have obtained this service, you simply dial your account number and identification code on a push-button phone, then read messages from the bank on your screen and punch in instructions to the bank.

■ Where Available.

An increasing number of banks, including most of the big money-center banks, offer their own computer service. Several independent services, such as CompuServe, offer home banking services that are accepted at many banks not having their own.

Many computers are compatible with most of these services. The Citibank and Chemical Bank services, for example, can be used with Atari, Apple, IBM, and Radio Shack TRS-80 equipment.

■ Specific Banking Services.

The specific features of different services vary considerably. Most permit you to check account balances, learn which checks and deposits have cleared, transfer funds between accounts, and pay bills. Some also provide a monthly or even year-to-date summary of account activity, a checkbook register that balances your checkbook, and individual check tracking by check number, amount, or date posted. In addition, some services offer brokerage services or electronic catalogues from merchants.

■ Charges.

Banks typically charge $5 to $12 monthly for basic home-banking services. They then assess additional monthly charges for use of such related services as trading stocks, supplying investment information, and managing your stock portfolio. Of course there is also the expense of the home computer system and phone usage.

■ Evaluation.

Home banking is available only to those with a personal computer. It cannot meet banking needs such as withdrawing cash or applying for a mortgage loan, and it is expensive if used principally to pay several bills each month.

On the other hand, home banking offers new information about your accounts and enables you to conduct some of your banking business much more conveniently. It can dramatically improve your ability to manage your bank accounts and plan financially. It is also relatively risk-free. Banks are liable for losses resulting from unauthorized withdrawals from your accounts. More than fifty thousand households already use home banking, and the number is growing.

Direct Deposit

Many banks, S & Ls, and credit unions offer direct deposit of pay checks and government checks. This entails an electronic transfer of funds from your employer, a welfare agency, or a Social Security office to your bank account. This service can increase the convenience and safety of your banking. No longer are you required to deposit checks in person or by mail. There is usually no charge for this service, although you should verify this with your bank. You should also inquire whether your bank places a hold on these funds.

The only controversial aspect of this service is a proposal to mandate direct deposit of government checks. Proponents argue that this procedure would substantially reduce theft and other losses of checks. But many recipients of welfare and Social Security checks are unhappy at the prospect of not receiving actual checks and being forced to do business with a bank.

$ ¢ $ ¢ $

¢ $ ¢ $ ¢

$ ¢ $ ¢ $

¢ $ ¢ $ ¢

3

Savings Options: An Overview

RECOMMENDATIONS

To allow for unexpected expenses, such as auto and home repairs, every consumer should have savings. You should keep at least three months' income in a savings account or money market fund that can be drawn upon immediately. If you are very conservative about financial planning, consider investing additional funds in savings vehicles such as certificates of deposit (CDs) or Treasury securities.

Your financial needs, age, willingness to assume risk, and income should influence your choice of savings options. But all consumers should evaluate the same general characteristics of these savings vehicles.

How to Evaluate Savings Options

The three fundamental factors you should consider in evaluating savings options are risk, liquidity, and yield. These factors are interdependent. There is no savings vehicle that offers low risk, high liquidity, and high yield. You must weigh the importance of each and make compromises.

■ Risk.

Risk is the possibility of receiving a lower yield than expected on an investment, or even losing all or part of your principal. The market rewards investors for bearing two basic types of risk. The first is risk of default: the possibility that the issuer of the financial instrument will be unable to make timely payments of interest or principal. You can avoid risk of default by putting your savings in accounts insured by the federal government or by purchasing securities issued by the federal government. Accounts at institutions insured by private insurance funds are not free from risk of default, as recent events in Ohio and Maryland have demonstrated.

The second type of risk is market risk: the possibility that the market value of your investment will decline because interest rates have increased. Market risk is a factor only in fixed-rate investments, and it depends on the length of time to maturity—the longer away the maturity date of a financial instrument, the greater its market risk. There are two reasons for this. First, the longer away the maturity date, the longer the time during which interest rates can rise. Second, increases in market interest rates have a greater impact on the prices of long-term securities than on short-term ones. Variable-rate savings options, such as variable-rate CDs and money market accounts, have no market risk.

■ Liquidity.

Liquidity measures the ease and cost of converting your investment into cash. The most liquid assets are cash and checking accounts, which are payable on demand. Savings accounts are slightly less liquid than checking accounts because the issuing institution can make account holders wait for their money. Somewhat less liquid than savings accounts are securities traded on the open market, such as Treasury bills. The least liquid assets are real estate, precious gems, and collectables. Although they are not negotiable, CDs issued by commercial banks, S & Ls, and credit unions are somewhat liquid, because most issuers are willing to redeem them for cash before they mature, albeit at a heavy cost to the owner. Only assets that are reasonably liquid are appropriate for use as savings vehicles.

■ Yield.

Yield is the rate of return on your investment on an annual basis. Factors affecting yield include the interest rate paid, the method used to compute the interest earned, and the frequency with which that interest is compounded.

In general, the more liquid a savings option, the lower its yield, all other things remaining equal. Also, the greater the risk of a savings vehicle, the greater the yield. Riskier assets also tend to be less liquid than those with lower risk.

In addition to risk, liquidity, and yield, the following factors contribute to the attractiveness of a particular savings option.

■ Taxability.

Interest paid by all of the savings vehicles discussed in this chapter are subject to federal income taxes, except those money market funds that invest only in tax-exempt securities. The interest earned on U.S. savings bonds and Treasury securities, however, is exempt from state and local income and personal property taxes. You should not seriously consider tax-exempt savings options unless you are in at least the 35% marginal income tax bracket.

■ Transaction Costs.

You may incur charges when buying or selling a financial instrument. These charges can be substantial. For example, Treasury security transactions of under $100,000 are considered odd lots and subject to a flat fee. Some banks and brokerage houses charge $50 or more for buying or selling a Treasury bill. Some have recently started imposing a fee for cashing the coupons attached to Treasury securities, which represent the interest they pay. You can substantially reduce these costs by shopping around for brokerage services or by buying Treasury securities directly from the Federal Reserve.

■ Institutional Fees.

Banks and S & Ls often charge a variety of fees for savings accounts, most commonly for inactive accounts and for accounts closed shortly after they are opened. Some institutions charge savers as much as two dollars a month to maintain accounts in which there has been no activity for at least a year. Others charge fees for savings-account withdrawals in excess of three per month.

■ Negotiability.

You can sell savings instruments that are negotiable to a third party. You cannot sell nonnegotiable instruments on the open market, but you can exchange them for cash at the issuing institution. All savings accounts and all CDs under $100,000 are nonnegotiable. Money market funds are negotiable. Treasury securities are negotiable, but U.S. savings bonds are not.

■ Expandability.

In general, once you purchase a bond or CD you cannot add to the principal, and may not even be able to reinvest the interest you earn. On the other hand, you can add to money market funds and money market accounts, but some accounts restrict additions (other than the reinvestment of interest) to amounts of $100 or more.

■ Convenience.

The convenience with which you can purchase a security or open and maintain an account varies among different savings vehicles, and different financial institutions offering the same vehicles. For example, some financial institutions will automatically deduct a set sum from your checking account and transfer it to your money market savings account each month; others will not.

■ Minimum Investment.

The minimum amount of money you need to purchase a savings vehicle varies widely. Ginnie Mae securities require minimum purchases of $25,000, whereas many banks will open a passbook savings account with an initial deposit of $10.

■ Other Services.

Many banks and some brokerage houses offer you a variety of free or low-cost services if you meet certain initial investment requirements. Some of these services can be valuable, such as free check printing. Others are nothing more than "bells and whistles," such as discounts on merchandise that is often available for the same price or less at discount stores.

Twelve Ways to Save

■ Regular Savings Accounts.

You can open these accounts at credit unions, commercial banks, and S & Ls. They require very small initial deposits, can be added to or withdrawn from in any amount at any time (at least in practice), and consequently are almost as liquid as cash.

The basic disadvantage of regular savings accounts is that they pay very low yields. Also, many banks impose a variety of charges against these accounts, which under certain circumstances can exceed the interest earned.

In general, you should try to avoid regular savings accounts. This type of account is only one step above a piggy bank. It may be a reasonable option for small savers, however, if the banking institution does not charge fees for low balances.

■ Money Market Deposit Accounts (MMDAs).

These accounts were introduced in December 1982 to allow banking institutions to compete for funds that were flowing into money market funds. Most federally insured institutions require a minimum deposit of $2500, but some require substantially less.

Institutions freely set interest rates. Rates can be changed daily, but generally are changed on a weekly basis. In August 1985, the yield on such accounts averaged 6.9%, slightly lower than the rate paid by money market funds.

In general, these accounts operate like regular savings accounts except that up to three third-party checks may be written and a total of six transfers made on them per month. Some financial institutions offer variations of these accounts that give you slightly higher yields at the cost of restricted access to your funds. An example of this type of account is a weekly maturity money market account that permits penalty-free withdrawals only on a specific day of the week.

■ Money Market Funds (MMFs).

Money market funds are offered by firms regulated by the Securities and Exchange Commission. They invest in short-term financial instruments such as Treasury bills, commercial paper (short-term unsecured obligations of major corporations), negotiable CDs issued by commercial banks, and bankers acceptances (a type of negotiable postdated check that is guaranteed by a major commercial bank). The yield of these funds changes daily, reflecting fluctuations in market conditions. The average yield paid in August 1985 was 7.4%.

Most of these funds require an initial deposit of $1000 to open an account, but after that, allow your balance to fall below that amount. The account can be added to or drawn from at any time, although transactions are generally limited to a minimum of $100. Some funds allow you to write checks against your balance, although most require that the check be for at least $500.

The basic disadvantage of the MMFs is that they are not insured by an agency of the federal government. Investors in such funds need not lose sleep over this, however. During 1983, after banks were allowed to offer high-yield savings accounts, 30% of the funds invested in MMFs was withdrawn, yet the funds had no trouble meeting their liquidity needs.

■ Certificates of Deposit (CDs).

Since October 1, 1983, certificates of deposit can be issued for any length of time and at any interest rate. Prior to that, severe restrictions were placed on the types of CDs regulated institutions could offer. In April 1982, credit unions were permitted to offer CDs on any terms.

As a consequence, shopping for a CD has become more difficult and time-consuming. The effective annual yield on CDs of the same maturity issued by competing financial institutions now varies widely. Because there are now important differences in yields depending on geographic regioins, savers would be wise to check yields being offered around the country in such publications as *Bank Rate Monitor* and *Barron's* before investing large sums in CDs.

CDs under $100,000 are not negotiable, and can be redeemed only at the issuing institutions. Federal regulations require that prematurely redeemed CDs be assessed a penalty of no less than one month's interest if they have a maturity length of one year or less, and three months' interest if they were issued with a maturity of over one year. Because most issuers of CDs charge much higher penalties, savers are advised to inquire before withdrawal about penalties. Moreover, institutions are under no obligation to redeem them before maturity, and some have refused to do so. Therefore, CDs are a nonliquid investment and should be purchased only if you are quite confident you will not need their funds until the maturity date.

■ Treasury Securities.

The U.S. Treasury finances our $2 trillion national debt by selling securities on the open market at competitively determined interest rates. You can purchase treasury securities directly through a Federal Reserve Bank or with the aid of a broker or bank. They are safe and liquid. Long-term Treasuries do carry a considerable amount of market risk, which increases with years to maturity (as is the case with all debt securities). Treasury securities are exempt from all state and local taxes except estate taxes. This can be of considerable benefit to you if you live in a high-tax state.

The Treasury issues three types of securities: bills, notes, and bonds. Bills are issued with maturities of fifty-two weeks or less, in minimum denominations of $10,000, with $5000 increments thereafter. Notes have maturities of one to ten years. The smallest note available with a maturity of less than four years is usually $5000. Notes with maturities of four years or more can be purchased in denominations of $1000. Bonds have maturities of ten to thirty years, and are issued in minimum denominations of $1000.

To purchase a Treasury bill directly from the Federal Reserve, you must submit a tender (which is nothing more than a special form) to that bank or one of its branches no later than 1:30 P.M. Eastern time the day of the auction. If you mail the form, you should send it directly to the Treasury. It must be postmarked no later than midnight of the day of the auction and received on the day of the auction. You should indicate on the tender that you are submitting a noncompetitive bid, and whether or not you want to have the funds reinvested when the bill matures.

Payment for the full face value of the bill must accompany the tender. You can make payment in the form of cash, certified personal check, check issued by a bank, S & L, or credit union drawn to the order of a Federal Reserve Bank or the Treasury, redemption check issued by the Bureau of Public Debt, or matured Treasury notes or bonds.

Since Treasury bills are issued at a discount from face value, you will have to send more than the cost of the bill with your tender. A refund check for the difference between the price of the bill and your payment will be sent to you shortly after the auction. Since you will submit a noncompetitive bid, the price you pay will be determined by the average of the accepted competitive bids. For example, if the average accepted competitive bid was 95.0 (a discount rate of 10% for twenty-six-week notes), you would receive a refund of $500 if you were buying a single $10,000 Treasury bill.

The procedure for purchasing Treasury notes and bonds is similar to the procedure for purchasing bills, but has some differences. You can pay with a personal check. There is no automatic reinvestment option. Since these securities are issued with coupons, you will have to send a small difference check to the Treasury if the average auction price exceeds 100.

■ U.S. Savings Bonds.

For years, economists have considered U.S. savings bonds to be a fraud perpetrated by the federal government to exploit the ignorance and patriotism of the American public. Although savings bonds have recently been made considerably more attractive than in the past, they are still not a good choice for most savers.

The new series EE bonds now earn the greater of either 7.5% or 85% of the average market yield of five-year Treasury notes, with the interest being compounded semiannually. This rate is earned only if the bonds are held for at least five years, however. Bonds held for shorter periods earn considerably less. A bond cashed in after only six months, for example, earns an annual yield of only 4%.

There are several advantages to U.S. savings bonds that may make them appropriate investments for some savers. First, the bonds can be purchased for as little as $25. Second, taxes on their earnings are not payable until the bonds are cashed. Finally, these bonds are exempt from state and local taxes.

■ Certificates of Accrual to Treasury Securities (CATS).

These are unit mutual funds that represent shares of ownership in a pool of Treasuries that have been stripped of their coupons. They are often called "zero coupon securities" (or bonds), since they are sold at a discount from face value and appreciate to face value at maturity. No interest is paid on CATS until they reach maturity.

However, federal and state income taxes must be paid each year on the imputed interest earnings. Investors who sell their CATS before they reach maturity receive their interest in the form of price appreciation.

CATS are traded on the New York Stock Exchange as bonds, and you can purchase them through a broker at nominal commission rates. CATS are free of risk of default, but are subject to market risk. If you sell a CATS long before it reaches maturity and interest rates have risen significantly since you purchased the security, the value of your CATS may be much lower than at the time of purchase.

■ Treasury Receipts.

These are the complement to CATS. They represent shares of ownership of a pool of coupons that have been stripped from Treasuries. The coupons represent the interest payments due on the securities. They are marketed by brokerage firms and have a wide range of maturities.

■ Ginnie Mae Securities (GNMA).

The Government National Mortgage Authority (Ginnie Mae) is part of the U.S. Department of Housing and Urban Development, and its securities are backed by the full faith and credit of the federal government. Ginnie Mae sells securities that represent ownership in a pool of mortgages, and guarantees the timely payment of principal and interest. GNMA securities generally carry higher yields than Treasuries, but are issued only in minimum denominations of $25,000.

Several mutual fund products make participation in GNMA securities possible for investors of more modest means. GNMA mutual funds, for example, are investment portfolios of GNMA securities which are professionally selected and managed by fund managers who reinvest the monthly income received from the securities. An investor in this type of fund realizes his or her return through the appreciation of the price of the shares.

GNMA unit trusts also represent shares of ownership in a professionally selected portfolio of GNMA securities. Owners of unit trusts receive interest and principal payments from the trust managers as they are earned, and no reinvestment is possible. When the trust reaches maturity in thirty years its value is zero, since all principal has been repaid. This type of investment is clearly not appropriate for individuals who are trying to build a nest egg, since you cannot accumulate assets in the trust easily. But it may be considered as an alternative to an annuity.

■ Cash Management Accounts (CMAs).

These new accounts combine a stock margin account with a money market fund account and a debit card (see Chapter 2). Brokerage firms charge as much as $100 per year for managing these accounts.

Many financial observers believe that the primary attraction of CMAs is snob appeal. Since many of them require a minimum opening balance of $20,000 or more, using a CMA is a way of telling the world that you have considerable liquid assets. CMAs are essentially a gimmick, and you would do well to avoid them, since each of their components can be acquired elsewhere for free. Further, once funds are deposited in a CMA, all decisions about how your money is invested are made automatically. For example, if you owe money on your margin account, all of your new deposits will be applied to pay off the balance on that loan, whether you want this to happen or not. In addition, having all of your assets in a CMA is likely to make you complacent about shopping for better yields elsewhere.

If you have a CMA, you should not use your debit card to make credit purchases. First, you lose the float you get when making a credit card purchase. More important, in case of a dispute, you lose the protection of the Fair Credit Billing Act and the Federal Trade Commission ruling that allows you to withhold payment from a third party that has purchased your note. You lose this protection because the margin credit extended by stockbrokers is exempt from these regulations.

■ Whole-Life Insurance.

Whole-life insurance combines insurance protection with a savings plan. Often marketed as an ideal savings vehicle by the insurance industry, whole-life insurance is an appropriate investment only for consumers in very high tax brackets. The tax advantage of buying a whole-life policy is a result of the fact that the earnings of the accumulated cash value are not subject to income tax until you cash the policy in.

There are several problems with whole-life insurance as a savings option. First, the cost of a dollar's worth of whole-life protection is so high that most consumers will end up buying too little insurance protection. Second, the rate of return on the savings component of most whole-life policies is lower than can be obtained elsewhere. Third, if you die before the policy is paid up your beneficiaries receive only the insurance, and lose the savings portion of the policy.

Whole-life insurance is sometimes promoted as a forced savings plan. If you are an individual who needs a forced savings plan, automatic payroll deductions for thrift plans or the purchase of U.S. savings bonds are a better alternative.

■ Individual Retirement Accounts (IRAs).

Individual retirement accounts allow individuals to make tax-deductible contributions of up to $2000 per year to their own retirement funds. Families with only one working spouse can contribute up to $2,250 a year, and two-earner couples can contribute up to $4000 per year. Funds in an IRA may be invested in anything, as long as the account is set up with a qualified trustee. In addition to being able to deduct IRA contributions from your income taxes, you do not have to pay taxes on earnings on your IRA until they are withdrawn, presumably during retirement, when you will be in a lower tax bracket. Even if this is not the case, the deferral of income taxes allows you to earn an effective rate of return much higher than you could earn in an ordinary savings plan.

Withdrawals from IRA accounts may begin as early as age 59½, and must begin by age 70½. If funds are withdrawn from an IRA prior to age 59½, they are subject to a 10% federal penalty, in addition to ordinary income taxes. Between ages 59½ and 70½, funds may be withdrawn at any rate the owner wishes. After age 70½, withdrawals may be made as quickly as desired, but no slower than a rate that would exhaust the funds by the end of your life expectancy as determined by an IRS table.

IRAs may be a useful tax shelter even for individuals who plan to withdraw their funds prior to reaching age 59½. For example, if you are in the 20% tax bracket, you would be better off with an IRA than an unsheltered savings program, assuming the IRA earns a rate of return of at least 10% and a withdrawal is not made for at least eight years.

Consumers who do not qualify for employer-sponsored tax-deferred thrift plans, tax-sheltered annuity plans or Keogh plans should seriously consider setting up an IRA account. Most individuals with IRAs have them at banks, S & Ls, or credit unions. However, many individuals choose to set up their accounts with stockbrokers or mutual funds. Mutual funds often offer the advantage of no management fees. A broker offers the consumer the advantage of having more flexibility in making investment decisions.

$ ¢ $ ¢ $

¢ $ ¢ $ ¢

$ ¢ $ ¢ $

¢ $ ¢ $ ¢

4

Options for Small Savers

RECOMMENDATIONS

If you cannot afford to set aside at least $1000 to open a money market savings account or an account with a money market fund, and you need access to your savings, you should consider a regular savings account. When shopping for a regular savings account at a bank, credit union, or S & L, look for the following features:

- At least 5.5% interest compounded daily or continuously.
- No or low minimum balance requirements for earning interest and avoiding account maintenance fees.
- No charges for withdrawals unless the number of free withdrawals is greater than the number you reasonably expect to make.

continued on next page

continued

- A day-of-deposit to day-of-withdrawal method of computing interest earnings, or its equivalent, average daily balance.
- Accessibility—nearness to your home or workplace, convenient hours, and twenty-four-hour teller machines.
- Federal insurance—your savings institution should be insured by an agency of the U.S. government.

Investigate credit unions when you consider opening a savings account. They are much more likely to have accounts that meet the above criteria than are banks or S & Ls. Further, they often offer free life insurance for the amount of the deposit—typically, up to $2000—and may offer higher yields than accounts at other financial institutions.

To keep things in perspective when shopping for a savings account, bear in mind that the difference in interest paid on a $1000 balance between the highest- and lowest-yielding accounts in our survey was only $16.70 a year. Factors such as accessibility and fees may prove to be more important to you than yield.

If you wish to save less than the $500 it generally takes to purchase a CD, want to save for long-term goals, and don't expect to need access to your savings for several years, consider purchasing U.S. savings bonds. You can buy them for as little as $25, and taxes on their earnings are deferred until the bonds are cashed.

Regular Savings Accounts

If you wish to save regularly but have only modest amounts of money to put aside, you have three options in today's marketplace: regular savings accounts, club accounts, and U.S. savings bonds. There are two types of regular savings: passbook accounts and statement savings. The principal difference between them is that with the former, your record is a passbook; with the latter, it is a monthly statement. Since banks are trying to phase out passbooks, some offer more favorable terms for statement accounts.

In 1976, we conducted an experiment in Cleveland to determine the yields available on ordinary savings accounts. Ten accounts, each with an initial balance of $1000, were opened on the same day at five commercial banks and five savings and loan associations. Identical transactions were made in each of the accounts on the same days. The accounts remained open for three months, and had low balances of $400. Nine different amounts of interest, ranging from zero to $9.63, were paid.

If the same experiment were performed today, it is certain that the range would be even greater. The account would earn no interest at some banks; fees would wipe out all interest earnings and result in a net cost of about $15 at Marine Midland in New York. On the other hand, the maximum the account could now earn at any bank or S & L is $10.10.

■ Method of Computing Interest.

A wide range of methods is used for computing the balance on which interest is paid on savings accounts. This factor, and the minimum balance needed to earn interest, are the most important determinants of the amount of interest earnings on savings accounts. Methods in common use include:

Low balance.

Under this method, interest is paid on the lowest balance in the account during the interest-crediting period. A bank using this system would pay no interest on an account open for over five months, regardless of the balance, if it paid interest quarterly and the account was opened after the start of the first quarter and closed prior to the end of the second quarter.

Collected balance.
Interest payments begin when the bank collects funds deposited to the account. Your deposit earns no interest until your check clears through the banking system. The delay can means loss of a day's interest on checks drawn on local banks to as long as two weeks on out-of-state checks. Many banks have no waiting period, so it is advisable to inquire about the bank's policy. Related to this policy is the holding policy, which makes depositors wait for access to their funds.

Last in, first out.
Withdrawals are deducted from the last deposit made. For example, if you deposited $500 two weeks ago and withdrew $200 today, the $500 deposit would be treated as a $300 deposit for interest-computation purposes.

First in, first out.
Withdrawals are deducted from the initial balance, and then from subsequent deposits, in the order made. For example, if you have an initial balance of $10,000, make a $2000 deposit on the fifteenth, and a $1000 withdrawal on the twenth-fifth, you would earn interest only on $9000 from the first through the fifteenth, and on $11,000 for the remainder of the month.

Some banks using the first-in, first-out method deduct withdrawals first from the first deposit made during the crediting period, then from subsequent deposits, and finally from the initial balance. In the above example, interest would have been earned on $10,000 for the first fifteen days of the month, and on $11,000 for the remainder of the month.

Day of deposit to day of withdrawal.
Interest paid on funds from the day they are deposited up until the day they are withdrawn. This is the method most favorable to the consumer, and the most common one in use.

Average daily balance.

This is essentially the same as day of deposit to day of withdrawal, so long as it is not modified with the words "available" or "collected." Interest is paid on the average of the balances in the account at the end of each day.

Grace days.

Some financial institutions will pay interest on funds retroactively if they are deposited within ten days of the start of the interest-crediting period. Some financial institutions will pay interest on funds to the end of a crediting period even if they are withdrawn as much as three days prior to the end of the period. Grace days generally are offered by institutions that use the low-balance method of computing interest, and hardly offset the enormous disadvantage of having such an account. However, several institutions that used the day-of-deposit-to-day-of-withdrawal method of computing interest also had grace days, a very desirable feature.

■ Effective Annual Yield.

Effective annual yield is the rate of return you will earn on your savings provided you do not incur service charges. There are three factors that determine effective annual yield: the interest rate, compounding of interest, and number of days in the bank year.

Interest rate.

At the time of our survey, regular savings accounts were among the few products still subject to rate restrictions. The maximum interest rate that could be paid on regular savings accounts at banks and S & Ls was 5.5%. Credit unions were not subject to this restriction. As of April 1986, the maximum interest rate restriction of 5.5% on regular savings accounts will be dropped. However, it is unlikely that a rate war will break out over regular savings accounts. The maximum yields on these accounts are likely to remain well below those paid on other savings vehicles.

Most institutions in our survey paid 5.5% interest on regular savings accounts. But one Philadelphia bank paid only 4% on passbook accounts.

Compounding of interest.

The compounding of interest is, in effect, the practice of paying interest on interest. The more frequently interest is compounded, the greater the effective annual yield.

Continuous compounding is the most favorable method, but it is essentially the same as compounding interest daily. An account with an average balance of $2500 will earn only one cent more per year under the continuous-compounding method as opposed to the daily-compounding method.

Number of days in the banking year.

Although there are 365 days in a calendar year, many banks operate on a 360-day year. Some banks and S & Ls divide the rate they pay by 360, but then pay interest for 365 days. This is called "compounding on a 365/360 basis," and is the most favorable method to savers. This factor can be more important than the frequency of compounding, as is demonstrated by Table 1.

Table 1
EFFECTIVE ANNUAL YIELD ON ACCOUNTS PAYING 5.25 AND 5.5% UNDER DIFFERENT COMPOUNDING & BANK-YEAR METHODS

	5.25% *365/365*	*5.25%* *365/360*	*5.50%* *365/365*	*5.50%* *365/360*
Semiannual	5.32%	5.39%	5.56%	5.65%
Quarterly	5.35	5.43	5.61	5.69
Continuously	5.39	5.47	5.65	5.73

As can be seen, the number of days in the bank year is as important as the frequency with which interest is compounded. Semiannual compounding on a 365/360 basis results in the same yield as continuous compounding on a 365/365 basis.

The easiest way to think of effective annual yield is in terms of cents per dollar. A 5.5% account compounded continuously on a 365/360 basis pays 5.73 cents per dollar, per year in interest.

■ Minimum Balance to Earn Interest.

Many banks and S & Ls have minimum balance requirements for accounts to earn interest. This minimum is applied either to the average balance in the account or to the daily balance. Under the first method, the balances at the end of each day in the interest-crediting period are added together and divided by the number of days: If the result is less than the minimum balance requirement, no interest is earned. Under the second method, if the balance in the account should ever fall below the minimum balance requirement, no interest is earned for the crediting period. A third variation of this requirement is to pay interest only on those days that the minimum balance requirement is met. The last method is the most favorable to most savers, while the second method is clearly the least favorable. The first method works out best for those balances that are usually above the minimum even though they occasionally fall below.

Our survey revealed many institutions that had minimum balance requirements of $1 or less. The highest minimum balance requirement was $500 at National Westminster in New York City (5¼% passbook account) and American National in Chicago. You should clearly try to avoid accounts with high minimum balance requirements.

A variation of the minimum balance requirement is the minimum earnings for crediting requirement. Under this method, interest will not be paid unless earnings meet a minimum level. One institution in our survey, for example, required that an account earn at least $1.50 per quarter for interest to be credited. Since the institution paid 5.5% on savings accounts, compounded daily on a 365-day basis, this minimum earnings requirement was comparable to a minimum average daily balance requirement of about $109.00.

■ Interest on Accounts Closed During Crediting Period.

Many financial institutions will not pay interest for a crediting period if the account is closed during that period. If you have such an account and are contemplating closing it, consider keeping a minimum balance in it until the end of the crediting period.

Accounts that pay interest to the date of closure are clearly preferable to ones that don't. However, since the amount of interest involved is generally small, and the loss of the interest is often avoidable, this is not a fatal flaw.

■ Interest Crediting Period.

Interest is generally credited either monthly or quarterly to savings accounts. The frequency of crediting interest is important only if there are minimum balance requirements or if interest is not paid when an account is closed prior to the end of the crediting period.

■ Fees and Charges.

Bank fees and charges have proliferated in recent years. Since rates on passbook accounts have been kept down by federal regulation while other interest rates have increased significantly, it would seem logical that fees on these accounts would have remained stable, or fallen. This has not been the case, however, and savings have been subject to ever-increasing fees by some financial institutions.

One reason for this may be that banks regard savings-account holders, as a group, the least financially sophisticated customers. Further, banks may reason they have the least to lose if such accounts are taken elsewhere, since savings-account balances are relatively low.

Free accounts for minors and senior citizens. Many financial institutions that ordinarily charge fees offer special no-fee accounts to minors and senior citizens. Qualified savers should look for accounts with this feature.

Account maintenance fees.

Many financial institutions levy charges against your account if certain minimum balance requirements are not met. Some banks apply maintenance fees if the account's balance falls below the minimum, while others do so only if the average daily balance reaches that level. The worst such fee we found was at a Chicago bank, which charged $5 for accounts whose minimum balance fell below $500 during the quarter.

Transaction fees.

Some financial institutions limit the number of withdrawals you can make from your savings account, and charge transaction fees for excess withdrawals. The highest fee we encountered was $3 for each withdrawal in excess of three per quarter, charged by Riggs Bank in Washington, D.C. A more typical charge was $1 per withdrawal in excess of three per quarter. Bay Bank in Boston charged .30 per withdrawal, regardless of the number made.

Many institutions do not assess transaction fees. If you intend to make more than one withdrawal per month, select an institution that does not assess these fees.

Inactive account fees.

Some banks and S & Ls charge fees against accounts if they are completely inactive for a period of time. Such fees are generally levied against accounts with low balances, and are often designed to wipe out the account balance before the funds have to be turned over to the state under abandoned-property laws. By doing this, institutions avoid the expenses associated with turning the money over to the state and can retain the funds for themselves.

For example, one bank in our survey, Republic Bank in Dallas, charged $1.50 per month after an account had been inactive for sixty days if the balance was below $50. These charges would wipe out a $49.50 account in less than three years.

Early closure fees.

A number of financial institutions charge a fee if your savings account is closed "early." The fee is generally modest, $3 or less, and is usually assessed only if your account is open ninety days or less. Some banks charge considerably more, and some charge the fee if you close the account within one year of opening. The highest fee from our survey was $25 for accounts closed within one year. This was charged by Marine Midland in New York.

Club Accounts

Christmas and vacation clubs are arrangements under which you make agreed-upon deposits to an account, usually every week or two. The savings institution then mails a check to you just before your holiday or vacation season. Club accounts are not as popular with bankers as they once were because of the relatively high cost of maintaining them.

These accounts usually pay the same rate as regular savings accounts, although some institutions pay more and others pay no interest at all. Some institutions will pay no interest in club accounts if the regular deposit schedule is not adhered to for the entire term the account is in effect.

Club accounts may be useful to you if you need incentives to save. Although you are under no obligation to make regular deposits, the club agreement may be sufficient to motivate you.

If you decide to open a club account, be sure that it pays at least 5.5% interest on a day-of-deposit-to-day-of-withdrawal basis. Also be sure that interest will be paid even if you do not meet your full club obligation, and that no fees of any kind are attached to the account.

U.S. Savings Bonds (Series EE)

For years, U.S. savings bonds were a poor choice for savers. They paid a lower rate of interest than savings accounts and were less liquid. Early redemption dates were spaced six months apart, and when savers cashed their bonds in early, they lost any interest they would have earned following an early redemption date.

The principal advantages of savings bonds were that they could be purchased in small denominations, and that they received more favorable tax treatment than ordinary savings. Savings-bonds interest is exempt from state and local taxes, and federal taxes on earnings are deferred until the bonds are cashed.

The basic change in savings bonds that makes them worth considering today is that they now pay a reasonable rate of interest. If you hold savings bonds for at least five years, they will earn 85% of the average yield on five-year Treasuries during their lifetime, with a minimum guaranteed rate of 7.5%. The rate of earnings is adjusted every six months.

If you cash your savings bonds in earlier than five years after issue, they will earn considerably less interest. If you cash them in after one year, they will earn 5.5%. Every six months the rate of earnings is increased by .25%, so a bond held two years will pay 6%. All interest is compounded semiannually.

Although savings bonds do not pay as much as long-term CDs, you should consider them if you are a small saver. They are particularly suitable if you can only set aside small sums of money on a regular basis for a goal in the distant future. However, if you cash a savings bond in less than eighteen months after it is issued, you will earn less interest on it than what you could have earned on a good regular savings account.

The tax advantages of savings bonds are unlikely to be of much use to most of the savers for whom the bonds are a reasonable savings alternative. This is because savings bonds are most appropriate for relatively low-income, low-tax-bracket savers. Further, if savers are not careful, the tax deferral feature may result in higher taxes. This would almost certainly be the case for a child who accumulates a significant number of savings bonds for, say, a college education. If all or many of the bonds are cashed in the same year, the accumulated interest that was deferred for tax purposes is likely to result in a significant income tax liability. To avoid this liability, declare the interest earned each year on your income tax statement.

You can take exception to the above rule if you are nearing retirement and wish to defer taxes on your interest earnings. If you have taken full advantage of other tax-sheltered savings programs, such as IRAs, savings bonds can be an appropriate savings vehicle.

C H E C K L I S T

Use this checklist when shopping for regular savings accounts.

Minimum balance to open __________

Minimum balance to earn interest __________

Interest rate __________

Annual percentage rate __________

Compounding __________

Basis for computing interest (e.g., day of deposit to day of withdrawal) __________

Grace days

- Beginning of period __________
- End of period __________

Interest creating period __________

Is interest paid if account is closed during crediting period? __________

Service charges

- Maintenance fee __________
- Minimum balance to avoid maintenance fee __________
- Transaction fee __________
- ATM transaction fee __________
- Minimum balance to avoid transaction fee __________
- Inactive account fee __________
- Time period to avoid inactive account fee __________
- Early closure fee __________
- Time period to avoid early closure fee __________

$ ¢ $ ¢ $

¢ $ ¢ $ ¢

$ ¢ $ ¢ $

¢ $ ¢ $ ¢

5

Certificates of Deposit

R E C O M M E N D A T I O N S

Certificates of deposit (CDs) are appropriate investments if you are willing to give up access to your funds, but unwilling to assume any risk of default. When purchasing a CD, aggressively seek out the highest yield, even if you find it in another city. CDs can be purchased and redeemed by mail, and require no attention in between.

Purchase CDs only from institutions insured by an agency of the federal government. These agencies are the Federal Deposit Insurance Corporation (FDIC) for banks, the Federal Savings and Loan Insurance Corporation (FSLIC) for Savings and Loans, and the National Credit Union Administration (NCUA) for credit unions. Avoid state and privately insured institutions. Also avoid uninsured instruments, such as subordinated notes, which are often marketed like CDs and sometimes issued by insured institutions.

continued on next page

continued

To maximize interest earned, purchase an investment option CD, in which interest is not paid out periodically, but accumulates until maturity. Shop for this type of CD by comparing the effective annual yields offered by different institutions. Be aware, however, that you must pay income taxes on the interest earnings of such a CD each year even though you will not receive the interest until maturity. The only exception to this rule is a CD with a maturity of one year or less. With these CDs, you can defer taxes until the interest is actually paid.

If you wish to receive interest earnings periodically, you should choose the income option CD. Under this option, monthly or quarterly interest payments will be made by the issuing institution, either by check or by transfer to another account. The only reliable way to shop for such a CD is to determine what the size of the monthly or quarterly interest payment will be.

If you do not want to lock yourself into a fixed rate of interest for a long period of time, you should consider variable-rate CDs. Most of these are designed for individual retirement accounts (IRAs). Many require very low initial investments and allow funds to be added to the principal at any time.

No matter what type of CD you choose, avoid those with very high early withdrawal penalties. Only CDs that charge the federal minimum penalties or straight replacement-cost penalties should be considered, unless an exceptional yield is promised.

Prior to the 1980s, consumers had little choice in selecting a CD. Banks and S & Ls were restricted by federal regulations as to the minimum size of their CDs, the rate they could pay, and other terms.

Today, CDs can be offered for any amount, for any time period, and for any rate of interest. As a consequence, and as a result of competition in the marketplace, many institutions will custom-design CDs for their customers. For example, an institution might be willing to offer a 920-day CD to meet customer demand.

This can be convenient if you are saving for a specific goal. You can either choose a CD that matures exactly when you will need the money or have a CD designed to be worth a desired amount when it matures.

If you are investing with a specific financial goal for the future, you can use a handy rule of thumb called "the rule of 70." To determine how long you must keep your funds invested for them to double, divide 70 by the interest rate paid. For example, if the effective annual yield on a long-term CD is 10%, it will take a little over seven years for the value of the CD to double (70/10 = 7).

■ Advantages and Disadvantages.

CDs offer several advantages over other long-term investment options:

- They are easy to buy, and involve no brokerage fees or other transaction costs.
- They are insured by an agency of the federal government for up to $100,000 per customer per institution if the issuing institution is insured.
- They are relatively easy to understand.
- There are rarely any management fees for IRA accounts set up as CDs.

But CDs also have disadvantages:

- They are quite nonliquid. Except when purchased from a broker who buys and sells them, a CD of less than $100,000 can be redeemed for cash only by the issuing institution. There are substantial penalties for early withdrawals, and the issuer is under no obligation to permit such withdrawals.

- Searching for the best yield on a CD can be time-consuming.
- Yields are generally somewhat lower than on riskier investment options.

Factors Affecting Yield

Yields on CDs vary widely, both from institution to institution and from city to city. In fact, our survey revealed one S & L, Fulton Federal in Georgia, that paid higher yields at its branches in some cities than in others.

Our survey revealed a range in yield on six-month CDs of almost four percentage points, which represents a difference in earnings of nearly $200 on a $10,000 deposit. The difference between the highest- and lowest- yielding three-year CD was over two percentage points. The highest-yielding three-year CD earned $700 more on a $10,000 deposit than the lowest-yielding three-year CD.

These differences reflect three factors: the interest rate, method of compounding, and number of days in the bank year. If you intend to allow interest to accumulate in a CD, you need concern yourself only with effective annual yield.

■ Rates.

Advertising practices of financial institutions make interest-rate comparisons difficult, because of the different ways in which interest rates can be stated. An example of potentially misleading advertising of interest rates was an advertisement that offered a simple interest rate of 15% on a five-year CD. The interest on this CD was not compounded, and as a result it would pay less than a CD with an annual rate of 11.5% compounded daily.

Most consumers should concentrate on effective annual yield. However, if you choose an income option CD, you should pay attention to rates, since income option CDs receive interest as it is earned, and it usually is not compounded. The only reliable way to compare income option CDs is to determine the size of the monthly or quarterly interest payments.

■ Compounding.

Compounding is the paying of interest on interest; it raises the effective annual yield of an investment. For a given rate, the more frequent the compounding, the higher the effective annual yield.

Here is a demonstration of the impact of compounding on the amount of interest earned on a $10,000, one-year CD paying 10%.

Type of Compounding	*Interest Earned*
Simple (no compounding)	$1,000.00
Semiannual	$1,025.00
Quarterly	$1,038.13
Monthly	$1,047.13
Daily	$1,051.56
Continuously	$1,051.71

The importance of compounding is illustrated by two institutions in our survey. The Bank of Boston offered a three-year CD paying 12%, compounded monthly; Security Pacific in Los Angeles offered a three-year CD paying 12.4%, compounded annually. The effective annual yield of the Bank of Boston CD was 12.68%, whereas the Security Pacific CD yielded only 12.4%. A $10,000 CD would have earned $107 more at maturity at the Bank of Boston.

■ Days in the Bank Year.

Although there are 365 days in a calendar year, there are only 360 days in the bank year at most institutions. Yet a few institutions pay interest for 365 days even though they only have 360 days in their bank year. This practice, called "compounding on a 365/360 basis," raises the effective annual yield of an account by a factor of 0.0139. For example, Talman Home Federal in Chicago offered an 11% interest rate, not compounded, for a one-year CD. Since it paid interest on a 365/360-day basis, the effective annual yield of the CD was 11.15% (11 × 1.0139 = 11.15).

This arcane practice is an artifact of the days when banks were subject to maximums on the annual rate of interest they could pay. Compounding on a 365/360-day basis was used to raise effective annual yields without exceeding the maximum annual rate.

Where to Find High-Yield CDs

A monthly newsletter, *Savers Rate News*, lists some of the highest-yielding CDs of different maturities. A year's subscription to this publication costs $49, and can be obtained by calling 1-800-447-0011 or by writing Circulation Manager-N, Savers Rate News, P.O. Drawer 52150, Miami, FL 33152-1250. Table 1 provides a sample.

Table 1
SAVERS RATE NEWS *HIGH-YIELD CDs (SEPTEMBER 1985)*

Institution-City State	*Phone-Contact*	*Minimum*	*Rate (%)*	*Yield (%)*
90 DAY CDs				
Capital S&L Phoenix, AZ	(602)274-3839 New Accounts	$1000	8.500	8.775
Commodore Sav Dallas, TX	(214)871-0005 Gywnne Autry	1000	8.500	8.770
Gill Sav San Antonio, TX	(800)531-4455 Alexis Hefley	500	8.250	8.720
Western Sav Dallas, TX	(800)526-7283 Lisa Hylbert	1000	8.250	8.720
Alliance S&L Houston, TX	(713)270-1212 New Accounts	2500	8.600	8.600
Audubon Fed S&L New Orleans, LA	(504)454-5300 Barbara Fowler	1000	8.250	8.600
Pacific Coast Sav San Fran, CA	(800)792-7283 Gloria Johnson	100	8.250	8.600
American Divers Costa Mesa, CA	(800)528-6666 Mike Blackshire	500	8.125	8.586
New Orleans FS&L New Orleans, LA	(504)947-0002 Robin Oddo	1000	8.125	8.569
Sun State Phoenix, AZ	(602)224-1107 Joanne Finn	2500	8.250	8.510
Eastern Sav Baltimore, MD	(301)358-3881 Donna Setters	1000	8.160	8.500

Institution-City State	Phone-Contact	Minimum	Rate (%)	Yield (%)
Laurel Sav Assn Laurel, MD	(301)725-2552 Mrs. Duck	2500	8.150	8.490
Summitt Sav Salt Lake City, UT	(800)531-8472 Customer Service	1000	8.125	8.463
Beneficial Nat'l Bk Wilmington, DE	(800)441-7084 Anne Sachtleven	1000	8.000	8.450
1st Nat'l Bk Wilmington, DE	(800)638-1520 Pat Renzi	500	8.120	8.450
South S&L Sledell, LA	(504)643-1300 Lynette Green	1000	8.000	8.450
United Sav West Vienna, VA	(703)281-7500 Dale Wallace	100	8.000	8.450
Mainland Sav Friendswood, TX	(800)231-0032 Jackie Resendez	2000	8.000	8.448
Hamilton Sav Bk San Fran, CA	(415)781-1910 Holly Salazar	1000	8.000	8.440
Guardian S&L Dallas, TX	(214)747-1664 Elaine Blankenship	2000	8.150	8.402
Pelican Hmstd Sav New Orleans, LA	(504)283-8883 New Accounts	2500	8.000	8.361
Sequoia S&L Baltimore, MD	(301)486-5228 Sandy Mitchell	2500	8.000	8.360
Enterprise Fed Morrero, LA	(504)340-1337 Sav. Counselor	1000	8.000	8.330
New South Fed Sav Bk Birmingham, AL	(800)547-8818 Rosalind Dowdell	1000	8.000	8.270
180 DAY CDs				
Hopkins S&L Baltimore, MD	(301)675-2828 Angela Jeffords	2500	9.000	9.420
Pacific Coast Sav San Fran, CA	(800)792-7283 Gloria Johnson	100	8.750	9.140
Capital S&L Phoenix, AZ	(602)274-3839 New Accounts	1000	8.750	9.041
Western Sav Dallas, TX	(800)526-7283 Lisa Hylbert	1000	8.500	9.000
Colonial Sav Houston, TX	(713)784-2260 Joanne Kennedy	1000	8.700	8.990
Commerce Sav Dallas, TX	(214)760-9245 Shirley Ruff	1000	8.650	8.930
Colonial Nat'l Bk Wilmington, DE	(800)441-7306 Maria Del Signora	2500	8.420	8.910
University Sav Houston, TX	(713)596-1000 Mr. Pat Claymore	2500	8.625	8.908

Table 1 continued
SAVERS RATE NEWS *HIGH-YIELD CDs (SEPTEMBER 1985)*

Institution-City State	*Phone-Contact*	*Minimum*	*Rate (%)*	*Yield (%)*
1st Fed S&L New Orleans, LA	(504)246-7111 Linda Bodin	500	8.500	8.871
Audubon Fed S&L New Orleans, LA	(504)454-5300 Barbara Fowler	1000	8.500	8.870
1st Nat'l Bk Wilmington, DE	(800)638-1520 Pat Renzi	500	8.500	8.870
American Divers Costa Mesa, CA	(800)528-6666 Mike Blackshire	500	8.375	8.861
Mainland Sav Friendswood, TX	(800)231-0032 Jackie Resendez	2000	8.375	8.861
Beneficial Nat'l Bk Wilmington, DE	(800)441-7084 Anne Sachtleven	1000	8.350	8.830
Alliance S&L Houston, TX	(713)270-1212 New Accounts	2500	8.800	8.800
Ben Franklin Sav Houston, TX	(713)940-6700 Customer Service	2000	8.500	8.775
Savings of America Dallas, TX	(214)386-8088 New Accounts	2500	8.500	8.775
Guardian S&L Dallas, TX	(214)747-1664 E. Blankenship	2000	8.500	8.774
Commodore Sav Dallas, TX	(214)871-0005 Gywnne Autry	1000	8.500	8.770
Paris Sav Dallas, TX	(214)239-0101 Cheryl Graves	500	8.500	8.770
Sun State Phoenix, AZ	(602)224-1107 Joanne Finn	2500	8.500	8.770
Eastern Sav Baltimore, MD	(301)358-3881 Donna Setters	1000	8.390	8.750
Meridian Sav Katy, TX	(713)392-1600 New Accounts	10000	8.750	8.750
Summitt Sav Salt Lake City, UT	(801)531-8472 Customer Service	1000	8.375	8.737
Gill Savings San Antonio, TX	(800)531-4455 Alexis Hefley	500	8.250	8.720
Hamilton Sav Bk San Fran, CA	(415)781-1910 Holly Salazar	1000	8.250	8.720
South S&L Sledell, LA	(504)643-1300 Lynette Green	1000	8.250	8.720
United Sav West Vienna, VA	(703)281-7500 Dale Wallace	100	8.250	8.720
Laurel Sav Assn Laurel, MD	(301)725-2552 Mrs. Duck	2500	8.300	8.653

Institution-City State	*Phone-Contact*	*Minimum*	*Rate (%)*	*Yield (%)*
Northpark Sav Dallas, TX	(214)363-8312 Jill Eslava	2500	8.625	8.625
Berkley Citizens FS Norfolk, VA	(800)841-6200 Ms. Dixon	2500	8.600	8.600
Enterprise Fed Morrero, LA	(504)340-1337 Sav. Counselor	2500	8.250	8.600
Metropolitan FS&L Bethesda, MD	(301)951-6500 Ms. Wells	2500	8.250	8.600

1 YEAR CDs

Institution-City State	*Phone-Contact*	*Minimum*	*Rate (%)*	*Yield (%)*
Hopkins S&L Baltimore, MD	(301)675-2828 Angela Jeffords	2500	9.500	9.960
Capital S&L Phoenix, AZ	(602)274-3839 New Accounts	1000	9.250	9.576
Savings of America Dallas, TX	(214)386-8088 New Accounts	2500	9.250	9.576
Western Sav Dallas, TX	(800)526-7283 Lisa Hylbert	1000	9.000	9.550
Great Amer Fed of Corinth-MS	(800)221-2591 Duane Ellis	2500	9.125	9.520
Pacific Coast Sav San Fran, CA	(800)792-7283 Gloria Johnson	100	9.000	9.420
Alliance S&L Houston, TX	(713)270-1212 New Accounts	1000	9.100	9.415
Severn S&L Annapolis, MD	(301)268-4554 Roanna Rusch	1000	9.000	9.380
Colonial Sav Houston, TX	(713)784-2260 Joanne Kennedy	1000	9.050	9.360
Alamo Sav of TX San Antonio, TX	(512)828-7171 New Accounts	500	9.000	9.310
Sun State Phoenix, AZ	(602)224-1107 Joanne Finn	2500	9.000	9.310
Ben Franklin Sav Houston, TX	(713)688-1087 Customer Service	2000	9.000	9.308
Guardian S&L Dallas, TX	(214)747-1664 E. Blankenship	2000	9.000	9.308
Gill Sav San Antonio, TX	(800)531-4455 Alexis Hefley	500	8.750	9.280
Hamilton Sav Bk San Fran, CA	(415)781-1910 Holly Salazar	1000	8.750	9.270
Continental Sav Angleton, TX	(800)231-1073 Janet Mather	500	9.250	9.250
1st Financial Bk New Orleans, LA	(504)581-9285 Deposit Counselor	1000	8.850	9.250

Table 1 continued
SAVERS RATE NEWS *HIGH-YIELD CDs (SEPTEMBER 1985)*

Institution-City State	*Phone-Contact*	*Minimum*	*Rate (%)*	*Yield (%)*
Lamar Sav Dallas, TX	(800)527-5182 Elaine Petrello	1000	9.250	9.250
Northpark Sav Dallas, TX	(214)363-8312 Jill Eslava	2500	9.250	9.250
Beneficial Nat'l Bk Wilmington, DE	(800)441-7084 Anne Sachtleven	1000	8.700	9.220
Commerce Sav Dallas, TX	(214)760-9245 Shirley Ruff	1000	8.900	9.200
1st Nat'l Bk Wilmington, DE	(800)638-1520 Pat Renzi	500	8.800	9.190
Financial Sav Dallas, TX	(214)630-1591 Richard Stokes	500	8.750	9.170
Sequoia S&L Baltimore, MD	(301)486-5228 Sandy Mitchell	500	8.650	9.170
Progressive S&L/Alham Bv Hls, CA	(213)859-8840 New Accounts	2500	8.850	9.150
1st Fed S&L New Orleans, LA	(504)246-7111 Linda Bodin	1000	8.750	9.143
1st Sav of E. TX Houston, TX	(713)975-1733 C. Housewright	500	8.750	9.143
Summitt Sav Salt Lake City, UT	(801)531-8472 Customer Service	1000	8.750	9.143
Audubon Fed S&L New Orleans, LA	(504)454-5300 Barbara Fowler	1000	8.750	9.140
Guardian Fed S&L Bridgeport, CT	(203)579-4764 Scott Zimmerman	1000	8.750	9.140
Metropolitan FS&L Bethesda, MD	(301)951-6500 Ms. Wells	1000	8.750	9.140
Vernon S&L Vernon, TX	(800)433-0970 Brenda	500	8.750	9.140
New Orleans FS&L New Orleans, LA	(504)947-0002 Robin Oddo	1000	8.750	9.110
United Bk San Fran, CA	(415)392-5400 Bill Peterson	500	8.600	9.110
18 MONTH CDs				
Hopkins S&L Baltimore, MD	(301)675-2828 Angela Jeffords	2500	9.750	10.240
1st Savings of Orange Orange, TX	(409)886-1918 Violet Johnson	500	9.000	9.696

Institution-City State	*Phone-Contact*	*Minimum*	*Rate (%)*	*Yield (%)*
Great Amer Fed of Corinth-MS	(800)221-2591 Duane Ellis	2500	9.250	9.625
Capital S&L Phoenix, AZ	(602)274-3839 New Accounts	1000	9.250	9.576
Gill Sav San Antonio, TX	(800)531-4455 Alexis Hefley	500	9.000	9.550
Hamilton Sav Bk San Fran, CA	(415)781-1910 Holly Salazar	1000	9.000	9.550
Yorkridge Calvert S&L Balt, MD	(301)843-4600 New Accounts	100	8.900	9.446
Audubon Fed S&L New Orleans, LA	(504)454-5300 Barbara Fowler	1000	9.000	9.420
Crescent FS&L New Orleans, LA	(504)482-5781 New Accounts	2500	9.000	9.420
Enterprise Fed Morrero LA	(504)340-1337 Sav. Counselor	1000	9.000	9.420
Metropolitan FS&L Bethesda, MD	(301)951-6500 Ms. Wells	1000	9.000	9.420
Vernon S&L Vernon, TX	(800)433-0970 Brenda	500	9.000	9.420
Charter Sav Corpus Christi, TX	(800)321-1479 New Accounts	100	9.000	9.416
1st Sav of E. TX Houston, TX	(713)975-1733 C. Housewright	500	9.000	9.416
Colonial Nat'l Bk Wilmington, DE	(800)441-7306 Maria Del Signora	2500	8.875	9.410
Sequoia S&L Baltimore, MD	(301)486-5228 S. Hobman	500	8.850	9.390
Chesapeake FS&L Baltimore, MD	(301)661-6700 Mr. Ciotta	500	9.000	9.380
Colonial Sav Houston, TX	(713)784-2260 Joanne Kennedy	1000	9.050	9.360
Security Sav Texarkana, TX	(214)832-8521 Terry Boston	500	9.010	9.320
2 YEAR CDs				
Gill Sav San Antonio, TX	(800)531-4455 Alexis Hefley	500	9.500	10.110
Western Sav Dallas, TX	(800)526-7283 Lisa Hylbert	1000	9.500	10.110
Northpark Sav Dallas, TX	(214)363-8312 Jill Eslava	2500	10.000	10.000
Severn S&L Annapolis, MD	(301)268-4554 Roanna Rusch	1000	9.570	10.000

Table 1 continued
SAVERS RATE NEWS *HIGH-YIELD CDs (SEPTEMBER 1985)*

Institution-City State	*Phone-Contact*	*Minimum*	*Rate (%)*	*Yield (%)*
Great Amer Fed of Corinth-MS	(800)221-2591 Duane Ellis	2500	9.500	9.930
Bright Banc Dallas, TX	(800)527-0184 Catherine Wilson	1000	9.450	9.910
Sunbelt Sav Dallas, TX	(800)527-5165 Customer Service	2500	9.500	9.844
New South Fed Sav Bk Birmingham, AL	(800)547-8818 Rosalind Dowdell	1000	9.500	9.840
PSFS Sav Bk Washington, DC	(202)537-8660 New Accounts	100	9.250	9.830
Continental Sav/Amer San Fran, CA	(415)861-1515 Andrew Bott	100	9.750	9.750
Alliance S&L Houston, TX	(713)270-1212 New Accounts	500	9.400	9.737
1st Sav of E. TX Houston, TX	(713)975-1733 C. Housewright	500	9.250	9.690
Pacific Coast Sav San Fran, CA	(800)792-7283 Gloria Johnson	100	9.250	9.690
South Boston Boston, MA	(617)268-2500 Mary Maroney	1000	9.250	9.650
Resource Ind. Bk Denver, CO	(303)399-1862 Sandy Pinkerton	1000	9.200	9.630
American Nat'l Baltimore, MD	(301)752-0400 Mr. Atkinson	500	9.300	9.629
Columbia S&L Beverly Hills, CA	(213)657-6303 Savings Dept.	1000	9.400	9.620
Nat'l Permanent Bk Washington, DC	(202)857-6700 New Accounts	500	9.150	9.580
Resource Sav Denison, TX	(800)835-8942 New Accounts	1000	9.250	9.580
Sun State Phoenix, AZ	(602)224-1107 Joanne Finn	2500	9.250	9.580
Capital S&L Phoenix, AZ	(602)274-3839 New Accounts	1000	9.250	9.576
Sav of America Dallas, TX	(214)386-8088 New Accounts	2500	9.250	9.576
30 MONTH CDs				
Hopkins S&L Baltimore, MD	(301)675-2828 Angela Jeffords	2500	10.000	10.560
Charter Sav Corpus Christi, TX	(512)854-1466 New Accounts	100	9.750	10.240

Institution-City State	*Phone-Contact*	*Minimum*	*Rate (%)*	*Yield (%)*
Great Amer Fed of Corinth-MS	(800)221-2591 Duane Ellis	2500	9.750	10.198
Gill Sav San Antonio, TX	(800)531-4455 Alexis Hefley	500	9.500	10.110
PSFS Sav Bk Washington, DC	(202)537-8660 New Accounts	100	9.500	10.110
Capital S&L Baltimore, MD	(301)752-6000 Ms. Rosenberger	500	9.500	10.100
United Bk San Fran, CA	(415)392-5400 Bill Peterson	500	9.410	10.010
Beneficial Nat'l Bk Wilmington, DE	(800)441-7084 Anne Sachtleven	1000	9.400	10.000
Guardian FS&L Bridgeport, CT	(203)579-4764 Scott Zimmerman	1000	9.500	9.970
Mainland Sav Friendswood, TX	(800)231-0032 Jackie Resendez	2000	9.375	9.970
Metropolitan FS&L Bethesda, MD	(301)951-6500 Ms. Wells	1000	9.500	9.970
1st Sav of E TX Houston, TX	(713)975-1733 C. Housewright	500	9.500	9.964
Chesapeake FS&L Baltimore, MD	(301)661-6700 Mr. Ciotta	500	9.500	9.960
Stockton Sav Ft. Stockton, TX	(915)336-8501 Jackie Bonda	500	9.500	9.960
U.S.A. Sav Rockville, MD	(301)231-9199 Colleen Williams	2000	9.500	9.960
American Nat'l Baltimore, MD	(301)752-0400 Mr. Atkinson	500	9.600	9.951
Yorkridge Calvert S&L Baltimore, MD	(301)843-4600 New Accounts	100	9.350	9.940
Continental FS&L Fairfax, VA	(800)255-2278 Linda Gillet	500	9.250	9.880
Western Gulf Bay City, UT	(800)457-0005 New Accounts	500	9.400	9.850
Broadview S&L Cleveland, OH	(216)447-1900 Norma Peters	500	9.500	9.844
2nd Nat'l Bk Severna Pk, MD	(301)544-2980 Cheryl Miller	250	9.500	9.844
Sunbelt Sav Dallas, TX	(800)527-5165 Customer Service	2500	9.500	9.844
Home Sav Bk Midland, TX	(800)426-4663 Cheryl Albin	No min.	9.500	9.843
Atlantic Perm. FS&L Norfolk, VA	(800)446-0200 Helena Fowler	500	9.500	9.840

Table 1 continued
SAVERS RATE NEWS *HIGH-YIELD CDs (SEPTEMBER 1985)*

Institution-City State	*Phone-Contact*	*Minimum*	*Rate (%)*	*Yield (%)*
New South Fed Sav Bk Birmingham, AL	(800)547-8818 Rosalind Dowdell	1000	9.500	9.840
3 YEAR CDs				
Home Owners Fed Boston, MA	(617)482–0630 Customer Service	500	10.050	10.679
South Boston Boston, MA	(617)268-2500 Mary Maroney	1000	10.000	10.470
Severn S&L Annapolis, MD	(301)268-4554 Roanna Rusch	1000	10.000	10.470
Western Sav Dallas, TX	(800)526-7283 Lisa Hylbert	1000	9.750	10.390
Mainland Sav Friendswood, TX	(800)231-0032 Jackie Resendez	2000	9.750	10.389
Home Sav Houston, TX	(713)965-8827 Pat Freeman	1000	10.000	10.381
New South Fed Sav Bk Birmingham, AL	(800)547-8818 Rosalind Dowdell	1000	10.000	10.380
Northpark Sav Dallas, TX	(214)363-8312 Jill Eslava	2500	10.250	10.250
Colonial Sav Houston, TX	(713)784-2260 Joanne Kennedy	1000	9.850	10.220
Great Amer Fed of Corinth-MS	(800)221-2591 Duane Ellis	2500	9.750	10.198
Bright Banc Dallas, TX	(800)527-0184 Catherine Wilson	1000	9.700	10.180
American Nat'l Baltimore, MD	(301)752-0400 Mr. Atkinson	500	9.750	10.112
Dominion Fed S&L McLean, VA	(800)368-2150 Maureen Berry	250	9.500	10.110
Gill Sav San Antonio, TX	(800)531-4455 Alexis Hefley	500	9.500	10.110
Resource Sav Denison, TX	(800)835-8942 New Accounts	1000	9.750	10.110
Sequoia S&L Baltimore, MD	(301)486-5228 S. Hobmann	500	9.500	10.110
Columbia S&L Beverly Hills, CA	(213)657-6303 Savings Dept.	1000	9.850	10.090
Alliance S&L Houston, TX	(713)270-1212 New Accounts	500	9.700	10.059
Nat'l Perm. Bk Washington, DC	(202)857-6700 New Accounts	500	9.550	10.020

Institution-City State	*Phone-Contact*	*Minimum*	*Rate (%)*	*Yield (%)*
Pioneer Sav Bk Clearwater, FL	(813)530-7600 New Accounts	2000	9.550	10.020
United Bank San Fran, CA	(415)392-5400 Bill Peterson	500	9.410	10.010

4 YEAR CDs

Institution-City State	*Phone-Contact*	*Minimum*	*Rate (%)*	*Yield (%)*
Home Owners Fed Boston, MA	(617)482-0630 Customer Service	500	10.050	10.679
PSFS Sav Bk Washington, DC	(202)537-8660 New Accounts	500	10.000	10.670
Resource Sav Denison, TX	(800)835-8942 New Accounts	1000	10.250	10.650
Beneficial Nat'l Bk Wilmington, DE	(800)441-7084 Anne Sachtleven	1000	9.950	10.610
Mainland Sav Friendswood, TX	(800)231-0032 Jackie Resendez	2000	9.875	10.529
Chesapeake FS&L Baltimore, MD	(301)661-6700 Mr. Ciotta	500	10.000	10.470
Great Amer Fed of Corinth-MS	(800)221-2591 Duane Ellis	2500	10.000	10.470
Columbia S&L Beverly Hills, CA	(213)657-6303 Savings Dept.	1000	10.150	10.410
Alliance S&L Houston, TX	(713)270-1212 New Accounts	500	10.000	10.381
Broadview S&L Cleveland, OH	(216)447-1900 Norma Peters	500	10.000	10.381
Home Sav Bk Midland, TX	(800)426-4663 Cheryl Albin	500	10.000	10.381
Atlantic Perm. FS&L Norfolk, VA	(800)446-0200 Helena Fowler	1000	10.000	10.380
New South Fed Sav Bk Birmingham, AL	(800)547-8818 Rosalind Dowdell	1000	10.000	10.380
Bright Banc Dallas, TX	(800)527-0184 Catherine Wilson	1000	9.850	10.350
Resource Industrial Bk Denver, CO	(303)399-1862 Sandy Pinkerton	1000	9.850	10.350
Household Bk Baltimore, MD	(301)962-5327 Savings Dept.	500	9.800	10.290
Loyola FS&L Baltimore, MD	(301)332-7000 New Accounts	500	9.800	10.290
American Nat'l Baltimore, MD	(301)752-0400 Mr. Atkinson	500	9.900	10.273
Meridian Sav Katy, TX	(713)392-1600 New Accounts	10000	10.250	10.250

Table 1 continued
SAVERS RATE NEWS *HIGH-YIELD CDs (SEPTEMBER 1985)*

Institution-City State	*Phone-Contact*	*Minimum*	*Rate (%)*	*Yield (%)*
Sunrise Fed Fairfax, VA	(703)352-8710 Ms. Laura Lynn	100	10.250	10.250
Enterprise Fed Morrero, LA	(504)340-1337 Sav. Counselor	1000	9.750	10.240
Guardian FS&L Bridgeport, CT	(203)579-4764 Scott Zimmerman	1000	9.750	10.240
Metropolitan FS&L Bethesda, MD	(301)951-6500 Ms. Wells	1000	9.750	10.240
Nat'l Penn Bk Washington, DC	(202)857-6700 New Accounts	500	9.750	10.240
5 YEAR CDs				
Eastern Sav Baltimore, MD	(301)358-3881 Donna Setters	5000	11.000	11.000
Gill Sav San Antonio, TX	(800)531-4455 Alexis Hefley	500	10.250	10.950
Columbia S&L Beverly Hills, CA	(213)657-6303 Savings Dept.	1000	10.650	10.930
New South Fed Sav Bk Birmingham, AL	(800)547-8818 Rosalind Dowdell	1000	10.500	10.920
Northpark Sav Dallas, TX	(214)363-8312 Jill Eslava	2500	10.875	10.875
Resource Sav Denison, TX	(800)835-8942 New Accounts	1000	10.400	10.810
Guardian FS&L Bridgeport, CT	(203)579-4764 Scott Zimmerman	1000	10.250	10.790
Great Amer Fed of Corinth-MS	(800)221-2591 Duane Ellis	2500	10.250	10.750
South Boston Boston, MA	(617)268-2500 Mary Maroney	1000	10.250	10.750
Home Owners Fed Boston, MA	(617)482-0630 Customer Service	500	10.050	10.679
Mountain Security Wytheville, VA	(800)368-3406 Janet Cornett	500	10.000	10.671
Yorkridge Calvert S&L Baltimore, MD	(301)843-4600 New Accounts	100	10.000	10.671
Sequoia S&L Baltimore, MD	(301)486-5228 Sandy Mitchell	2500	10.000	10.670
Mainland Sav Friendswood, TX	(800)231-0032 Jackie Resendez	2000	10.000	10.669
Atlantic Perm. FS&L Norfolk, VA	(800)446-0200 Helena Fowler	500	10.250	10.650

Institution-City State	Phone-Contact	Minimum	Rate (%)	Yield (%)
Home Sav Houston, TX	(713)965-8827 Pat Freeman	1000	10.250	10.650
Household Bk Baltimore, MD	(301)962-5327 Savings Dept.	500	10.100	10.630
Centrust S&L Miami, FL	(305)376-5456 Customer Service	500	10.090	10.620
Colonial Sav Houston, TX	(713)784-2260 Joanne Kennedy	1000	10.200	10.600
Alliance S&L Houston, TX	(713)270-1212 New Accounts	500	10.200	10.597
American Nat'l Baltimore, MD	(301)752-0400 Mr. Atkinson	500	10.200	10.596
Westview FS&L Baltimore, MD	(301)747-6200 Mrs. Grammer	100	9.900	10.560
Nat'l Perm. Bk Washington, DC	(202)857-6700 New Accounts	500	10.000	10.520
Peoples Bk Bridgeport, CT	(203)579-7436 Donna Harkins	1000	10.000	10.520
Pioneer Sav Bk Clearwater, FL	(813)530-7600 New Accounts	2000	10.000	10.520

LONG TERM CDs

Institution-City State	Phone-Contact	Minimum	Rate (%)	Yield (%)
Alliance S&L Houston, TX	(713)270-1212 New Accounts	500	11.100	11.571
Columbia S&L Beverly Hills, CA	(213)657-6303 Savings Dept.	1000	10.950	11.250
New South Fed Sav Bk Birmingham, AL	(800)547-8818 Rosalind Dowdell	1000	10.650	11.080
Pacific Coast Sav San Fran, CA	(800)792-7283 Gloria Johnson	100	10.500	11.070
Great Amer Fed of Corinth-MS	(800)221-2591 Duane Ellis	2500	10.443	10.960
Sequoia S&L Baltimore, MD	(301)486-5228 Sandy Mitchell	2500	10.250	10.950
Home Sav Houston, TX	(713)965-8827 Pat Freeman	1000	10.500	10.920
Lincoln S&L Los Angeles, CA	(213)475-4594 Mr. Razavi	500	10.300	10.848
Resource Sav Denison, TX	(800)835-8942 New Accounts	1000	10.400	10.810
Colonial Sav Shawnee Mission, KS	(913)648-6500 Cynthia Synder	500	10.340	10.750
Overland Park S&L Overland Pk, KS	(913)642-3030 C. Katsanponess	500	10.230	10.750

Table 1 continued
SAVERS RATE NEWS *HIGH-YIELD CDs (SEPTEMBER 1985)*

Institution-City State	*Phone-Contact*	*Minimum*	*Rate (%)*	*Yield (%)*
Home Owners Fed Boston, MA	(617)482-0630 Customer Service	500	10.050	10.679
United Bk San Fran, CA	(415)392-5400 Bill Peterson	500	10.000	10.670
Mainland Sav Friendswood, TX	(800)231-0032 Jackie Resendez	2000	10.000	10.669

RATES SUBJECT TO CHANGE WITHOUT NOTICE.
CONTACT INSTITUTION BEFORE INVESTING.

Other Features of CDs

■ Mailing of Interest and Interest Transfers.

If you purchase a CD for income, there are two convenient ways to receive the interest earnings: have interest checks mailed to you or have the interest transferred to another account at the same institution. If you have a short-term CD that does not compound interest, you should have the interest mailed to you as frequently as possible and deposit the proceeds in an interest-bearing account, since you will earn no interest on the funds accumulating in your CD.

Of the institutions we surveyed, all but one offered both options on CDs with maturities of one year or more. (Wells Fargo in California offered only the interest transfer option.) The great majority of institutions also offered both options on six-month CDs. Many institutions, however, offered these options only on CDs above a minimum amount. The highest minimum we found was $100,000 for monthly interest mailing or transfer, at First American in Washington, D.C. The next-highest minimum was only $10,000, and typical minimums were $5000 for monthly payments and $1000 for quarterly payments.

■ Notice of Maturing CD.

Look for institutions that will send you a notice when your CD is about to mature. It is easy to forget the exact maturity date of a long-term CD, and there may be serious consequences for letting a matured CD sit, as explained below.

Most institutions automatically send notice when a CD is about to mature. About a quarter of the institutions in our survey sent notices only if the rates paid on their CDs had changed since the CD was first issued. This is almost certain to be the case in today's marketplace.

Unless you instruct an institution to the contrary, most will automatically renew your CD for the same term at the current rate when it matures. Many will allow you to elect an automatic renewal option at the time you purchase the CD. Although this may seem to be a desirable feature, it has two disadvantages: you may unknowingly receive a lower yield than you could earn elsewhere; and if your CD has already been renewed at a time when you need the principal, you will be assessed early-withdrawal penalties.

Most institutions that do not automatically renew maturing CDs pay no interest on the deposited funds after the maturity date. One exception is Bay View Federal in San Francisco, which pays 5.25% on the balance until the funds are claimed.

■ Renewal of Maturing CDs.

Redeem your CD on the day it matures and reinvest your funds, if appropriate, at the highest yield you can find at an insured institution. If possible, arrange to have the proceeds from a maturing CD transferred to an interest-bearing account on the maturity date.

■ Early-Withdrawal Penalties.

Federal regulations require that banks and S & Ls charge a substantial penalty for early withdrawals from CDs. The minimum is one month's simple interest on the amount withdrawn for CDs with a maturity of one year or less, and three months' interest for those with longer terms. These penalties can be waived at the option of the issuer.

Early-withdrawal penalties can exceed the interest earnings on your account. If this happens, you will not receive any interest, and will lose part of your principal as well.

Less than a third of the institutions we surveyed charged the federal minimum penalties. Most charge substantially more, and some use replacement cost when that is more than the federal minimum as the basis for their penalties.

The most common method for assessing replacement cost is to compute the additional interest cost to the institution of issuing a new CD for the term remaining on the CD being cashed in early. For example, if you want to cash in a three-year 12% CD after one year, and the current rate for two-year CDs is 14%, the replacement cost would be 4% of the face value (2% × two years). On a $10,000 certificate, your penalty would be $400. This is $100 more than the federal minimum penalty of three months' interest.

A replacement-cost penalty is equitable inasmuch as it compensates the institution for the additional expense involved in replacing funds the depositor had committed for an agreed-upon time. However, institutions using replacement-cost penalties should not also subject their depositors to federal minimums. In fact, we believe institutions should pay a bonus for early withdrawals if interest rates have fallen, since the issuer can replace the funds at a lower interest rate. The only institution that approaches this ideal is University Savings in Houston, which pays an interest-rate bonus if rates have fallen, but limits the size of the bonus to the federal minimum penalty.

Most institutions that do not use replacement cost and/or federal minimums in computing early-withdrawal penalties charge three months' interest for CDs with terms of one year or less, and six months' interest on CDs with terms of over one year. These are the old federal minimums. Some institutions, however, assess penalties that are often even harsher than the old federal penalties. For example, Harris Bank in Chicago charges the federal minimum plus replacement cost. Three institutions—Broadview Savings in Cleveland, World Savings in Oakland, and First Bank of St. Paul—charge penalties of six months' interest on CDs with maturities of one year or less, and nine months' interest on longer-term certificates. Bank of America in California charges a penalty of three months' interest on CDs with terms of one year or less and six months' interest on longer-term CDs. In addition, for CDs with maturities of over one year, the interest paid on the funds on deposit for over six months is reduced to 5.25%. Table 2 demonstrates these specific early-withdrawal penalties.

As the certificate gets closer to maturity, the replacement-cost penalty will fall for any given interest rate, and the Bank of America penalty will rise. For example, if the CD is cashed in after eighteen months, the replacement cost would be $300 if interest rates have risen to 14%, while the Bank of America penalty would be $1,275.

If you are considering cashing in a CD early, you should explore other ways to raise the money you need. One alternative is to borrow funds from the issuer of the CD, using the certificate as collateral. (See Chapter 8 on installment loans.) Such loans are sometimes available at an interest rate only one or two percentage points above

Table 2
EARLY WITHDRAWAL PENALTIES ON A $10,000 THREE-YEAR 12% CD CASHED IN AFTER ONE YEAR

Type of Penalty or Name of Institution	*Penalty if Rates Rise to 14%*	*Penalty if Rates Fall to 10%*
Federal minimum	$300	$300
Replacement cost when greater than federal minimum	400	300
Old federal minimum	600	600
Harris Bank	700	300
First Bank, St. Paul	900	900
Bank of America	938	938

the rate being paid on the CD. In some cases, especially when the CD is close to maturity, an installment loan or even a cash advance on a credit card will be less costly than cashing in a CD early.

Variable-Rate CDs

Three-quarters of the institutions we surveyed offered some sort of variable-rate CD, although most issued them only for IRA accounts. IRA CDs generally require very low initial deposits—as little as $1; typically, $100—and allow or require additional investments during the term of the certificate. The highest initial deposit we found for an IRA was $500. Minimum additions ranged from a low of $1 to a high of $100.

Non-IRA variable-rate CDs require substantial initial investments, typically $500. The highest initial investment we found was $1000 at the Bank of New England in Boston.

The typical term for a variable-rate CD is 18 months. Some institutions offer much shorter terms; Bay Bank in Boston offered a three-month term. Several offered longer terms; Mellon Bank in Pittsburgh issued them for as long as ten years.

The majority of institutions offering variable-rate CDs changed the rate monthly. Some adjusted rates weekly, and Fidelity Federal in California changed rates daily.

At most institutions interest-rate adjustments on variable-rate CDs are left to the discretion of management. This is not favorable to consumers, and it is best to avoid such accounts. Other institutions tie the rate paid to rates paid on other products they offer. For example, several banks tie the rate to the interest rate they pay on newly issued six-month CDs. The most favorable formula we found was used by American Savings and Loan in California, which tied the rate of their two-year variable-rate CDs to the yield on thirty-month Treasury notes. Since thirty-month Treasury notes almost always have a higher yield than shorter-term issues, depositors at American would normally earn higher rates of interest than those who had deposits at other institutions.

Most other institutions surveyed set the rate on their variable-rate CDs according to either the thirteen-week or twenty-six week Treasury bill auction rate. The auction rate is a discount rate, and is considerably less than the actual yield of these instruments. Several institutions paid a premium of as much as one percentage point above the auction rate. The most favorable practice we found among those institutions was at Loyola Federal S & L in Baltimore. They set their rate each month by taking the higher of either the most recent twenty-six-week Treasury bill auction rate or the average of the last four such auctions, and then adding one percentage point. For example, if the average discount of the last Treasury auction was 7%, these institutions would pay 8%.

In brief, look for a variable-rate CD with a high yield that is indexed to some federal interest rate. Such an index will prevent the bank from arbitrarily lowering the rate.

Other Types of CDs

Several institutions have recently started to offer what can best be described as modified variable-rate CDs. Two examples are the "One Way CD" offered by Fidelity Federal in California and the "Rate Exchange Account" offered by Dollar Dry Dock in New York City.

Fidelity's One Way CD is a six-month fixed-rate CD that can be renewed at the same rate at which it was issued. If rates rise, depositors can either renew at the higher rate or withdraw their funds. If rates fall, the CD can be renewed at the original, higher, rate.

Dollar Dry Dock's Rate Exchange Account is a fixed-rate CD issued for terms of two to five years. At the end of eighteen months, or twenty-four months for CDs of three years or more, the depositor may exchange the fixed-rate CD for one with a variable rate without changing the maturity date of the certificate. This is an attractive option if rates rise substantially.

The unique features of these two accounts favor the consumer. But they are worth, at most, only between .25 and .50 percentage points on the effective yield.

Merchandise Offers

Financial institutions sometimes offer merchandise instead of interest on CDs, or merchandise in return for accepting a lower rate of interest than is available elsewhere. Often advertised as "gift" programs, most merchandise deals are not advantageous to the depositor. Among other factors, the careful analysis required to determine the true value of the merchandise offer is troublesome and extremely complex.

For example, in July 1985 Republic Bank in New York City offered a nineteen-inch Sony TV (model number KV1957R) instead of interest on a $2,300 twenty-three-month CD. The TV was a discontinued model that had a low retail price, less than $400. Emigrant Savings Bank in New York offered a two-year CD yielding 9% on the same day the Republic offer was made. Assuming the same yield could be earned for a twenty-three-month CD at Republic, the consumer would give up $422.12 in interest available at maturity in exchange for the TV. The discounted present value of the forgone interest, using a 9% discount rate, was about $360. So the Republic offer was reasonable, but unspectacular.

In general, you should consider the purchase of a product and the purchase of a CD as two separate decisions, and try to obtain the best possible deal on both of them. You can rarely do this by accepting a merchandise offer with the purchase of a CD.

C H E C K L I S T

Use this checklist when shopping for CDs.

Minimum size ____________

Interest rate ____________

Method of compounding ____________

Days in bank year ____________

Yield ____________

Are additions allowed

Without extending term? ____________

With extending term? ____________

Size of quarterly or monthly check (income option only) ____________

Notice of maturing CD sent ____________

If no instructions at maturity, what is done? ____________

Early-withdrawal penalty ____________

For Variable-rate CDs

Frequency of rate adjustment ____________

Is rate tied to an index? ____________

Minimum addition (if available) ____________

6

Money Market Deposit Accounts and Money Market Funds

RECOMMENDATIONS

If you have more than $1000 in savings and want ready access to your money, keep your savings in either a money market fund (MMF) or a money market deposit account (MMDA). The choice between the two is a difficult one. MMFs offer a somewhat higher yield, provide unlimited check writing (usually subject to a minimum check size), and are generally free of fees, but are not federally insured. MMDAs offer only limited check-writing privileges (three checks per month) and often charge fees, but are more accessible than MMFs, and carry federal insurance.

Since MMDAs pay high interest only if certain balance requirements are met, savers choosing an MMDA should seek

continued on next page

continued

one that either uses average balance during the month to determine if the requirement is met, or pays high rates for those days that the minimum balance is met. You should seek out accounts that have no service or transaction fees, and no minimum transaction sizes, and compute interest on a day-of-deposit-to-day-of-withdrawal basis.

Savers who choose MMFs have a broader range of choices. The ideal MMF has conservative investments, low transaction minimums, offers a toll-free number for transfers, and has no fees. The cost of greater safety and convenience may be a slightly lower yield than other funds pay. When shopping for an MMF, compromises often must be made.

If you have significant amounts to save, two liquid savings options that pay competitive interest rates are available to you: money market funds and money market deposit accounts at banks and S & Ls. Most MMFs require a minimum opening balance of $1000, although a few require substantially more—as much as $50,000. The smallest MMDAs available generally require a minimum deposit of $2500, although a few require only $1000.

When first authorized in December 1982, MMDAs were required by federal regulation to have balances of at least $2,500. In 1985, this minimum was lowered to $1000, and from April 1986 there will be no minimums. However, few institutions lowered their minimum deposit requirements in 1985, and it is unlikely that many will lower their requirements in 1986.

Although MMFs are quite safe, because they are not federally insured there is some risk. At least one firm in our survey offered a money market fund with private insurance. MMDAs, like other deposits at banks and S & Ls, are insured by agencies of the federal government for up to $100,000.

Money Market Deposit Accounts (MMDAs)

Since December 1982, federal regulations have allowed banks, S & Ls, and credit unions to offer MMDAs to compete effectively for the more than $200 billion that had flowed into money market funds during the late 1970s and early 1980s. Institutions may pay any interest rate they wish on MMDAs and change the rate as often as they desire without informing the depositor. On average, the yield on these accounts is slightly below the yields that can be earned from MMFs.

MMDAs are subject to restrictions mandated by federal regulations. Although check writing and automatic transfers are allowed, there are limits to the number of such transactions. No more than a total of six such transactions is allowed in any given month, with no more than three of these transactions in the form of checks. If these totals are regularly exceeded, the regulators consider the account to be a transactions account rather than an MMDA, and the issuing institutions are subject to high reserve requirements on the balances in the accounts.

Banks and S & Ls have taken several different steps to discourage or prevent customers from exceeding the limits on checks and automatic transfers. Most charge a hefty fee for excess transactions. The typical fee is between $5 and $10; however, several banks charge $20, and Lloyds Bank in California charges $25. On the other hand, St. Louis Federal charges only $1. Others simply close the consumer's account if excess transactions continue. Still others refuse to honor checks written in excess of the limit, and refuse to make preauthorized or telephone transfers. As an additional penalty, the depositor is usually charged a bounced-check fee. One bank, Continental in Philadelphia, simply drops the rate on the account to 5¼% if excess transactions occur. This could be quite costly.

Since there is always the chance you may inadvertently exceed your check limit, avoid accounts that either charge high excess-transaction fees or dishonor checks written in excess of the limit.

If you regularly exceed transaction limits, you should seriously consider an MMF or a SuperNOW account as alternatives.

Factors to Consider in Choosing an MMDA

■ Interest Rates.

The rate of interest paid on MMDAs varies widely. Our survey revealed a range of 3.4 percentage points. The highest rate we found was 10.4% at the Bank of Boston, and the lowest rate was 7% for accounts under $10,000 at Mercantile Bank in St. Louis. However, since the rate of interest paid on MMDAs changes frequently, sometimes every day, it is difficult to compare accounts by looking at the yield offered on any given day. An additional complication results from the fact that financial institutions are free to set rates on MMDAs at any level they choose. There is no guarantee that banks and S & Ls paying high rates for several weeks, or even months, will not suddenly lower them below those paid by most other institutions.

Some financial institutions do tie their rates to an index, which offers some assurance that their rates will remain competitive. St. Louis Federal pays .25% above the average rate paid by the ten largest general-purpose money market funds available to the general public. This makes the yield on their MMDA one of the highest in the United States. Yet even institutions that currently tie their rates to an external index are not obligated to continue doing so.

Institutions usually compound interest monthly on MMDAs. A few compound interest daily. These may pay a higher effective annual yield than rival institutions that are paying a higher interest rate but only compounding interest monthly. The difference is minor, however. For example, an account that pays 10% compounded daily will yield 10.52%, while one that pays a rate of 10% compounded monthly will yield 10.47%. This is a difference in earnings of $5 per year on an account that had an average balance of $10,000.

The best way to shop for rates is to ask institutions to provide you with the average yield or average rate of their money market accounts over the past year. But remember that a yield at one bank may not be comparable to a rate at another. Also keep in mind that small differences in yields do not mean much unless large sums are involved. A difference of .25% on a $5000 average balance is only $12.50 a year.

Some financial institutions offer higher rates, sometimes called "bonuses," on money market accounts with large balances. In the Detroit area, for example, Down River Federal and First Federal of Michigan will pay .25% more for accounts with average balances of $20,000 or more. National Bank of Detroit adds .25% for balances above $10,000; Standard Federal pays higher rates for accounts with balances of $25,000 and still higher rates for balances over $50,000.

If you are a saver with a large balance, determine which institutions offer higher rates for high balances and compare rates, including bonuses, among competing institutions. But remember that the bonus rate of one institution may be below or the same as the regular rate at a competing institution. On July 17, 1984, for example, Down River's bonus rate was 8.75%, which was the same as the regular rate at First Federal and the National Bank of Detroit. In New York City, Manufacturers Hanover Trust paid a bonus rate of 10% for balances above $15,000, while Citicorp offered a regular rate of 10.10%. Both institutions compounded interest daily.

■ Minimum Balance to Earn Higher Interest Rate.

Most financial institutions refuse to pay market rates on MMDAs unless a balance of $2500 is maintained. Some institutions require even higher balances, as much as $5000 in our survey.

Institutions differ as to how they treat balances that fall below their minimums. The two most common policies are: pay high rates for the entire month if the average balance in the account is at least $2500; and pay high rates for days on which the balance is above $2500, but only 5.25% when the balance is lower. If you have balances close to the minimum that occasionally drop significantly below that level, seek out an account using the second method. If you have much higher average balances that only occasionally drop below the minimum, you will be better off with an account using the first method.

Four other policies are used by institutions:

If the balance ever falls below $2500 in a month, the entire balance earns only 5.25%. Union National Bank in Pittsburgh and Allied Bank in Houston used this method.

If the minimum balance in the account falls below $2500, or if the average balance falls below some higher figure, interest is reduced to 5.25%. This average balance was $5000 at National Westminster in New York and $4000 at First of America of Detroit.

If the average balance falls below $2500, no interest is paid. Continental Illinois was among the banks following this policy. American National Bank, also in Chicago, required an average balance of $5000 to earn interest.

A variation of the above is to pay money market rates on balances above a certain minimum, 5.25% on balances between that level and a second minimum, but nothing if one minimum balance falls below the second minimum. Pittsburgh's Union Trust's standard money market account paid 5.25% on those days the balance fell below $2500, but nothing on days when it was below $1000.

■ Method of Computing Interest.

Several methods are used to compute balances on which interest is paid. These methods generally affect earnings far more than the method of compounding.

Day of deposit to day of withdrawal.

Interest is earned on funds as soon as they are deposited, no matter what form the deposit takes (cash, check from the same bank, check from another bank). They continue to earn interest up to, but not including, the day they are withdrawn. The average daily balance method is essentially identical to this method. This is the most favorable method available.

Daily collected balance (also called ***investable balance***).

Deposits of cash and checks drawn on the same bank begin to earn interest as soon as they are deposited. Checks drawn on other banks do not begin to earn interest until the bank sets provisional credit for the item. This generally takes one or two business days.

Low balance.
Interest is paid only on the lowest balance in the account during the computing period.

Modified low balance.
This is not a term financial institutions use, but is descriptive of a practice that has no formal name. Under this method, if the minimum balance in the account is above $2500 (or in some cases $5000), the balance for interest purposes is computed using either the day-of-deposit-to-day-of-withdrawal or daily collected balance method. If it ever falls below that level, no interest is earned. This effectively means the institution is using the low balance method for accounts when minimums are not met.

Last in, first out.
Withdrawals are deducted from the last deposit. For example, if you made a deposit of $2000 on the fifteenth of the month and withdraw $1000 on the twenty-fifth of the month, the withdrawal would be deducted from your $2000 deposit, and you would earn no interest on the $1000 that was on deposit from the fifteenth to the twenty-fifth.

First in, first out.
Withdrawals are deducted from the initial balance, and then from subsequent deposits in the order made. For example, if you have an initial balance of $10,000, make a $2000 deposit on the fifteenth, and a $1000 withdrawal on the twenty-fifth, you would earn interest on only $9000 from the first through the fifteenth, and on $11,000 for the remainder of the month.

■ Interest on Accounts Closed during Crediting Period.

About half the institutions we surveyed did not pay interest on accounts closed during a crediting period, which is always a month, but not necessarily a calendar month. Some did so only at the personal request of the customer, and one, University Savings in Houston, paid only if there were no excess transactions in the account and the average balance was $2500.

If you are planning to switch accounts from an institution that does not pay interest when an account is closed, you should wait until the end of the interest-crediting period to do so. Any advantages of your new account are likely to be more than offset by the interest lost on your old account.

Transactions in MMDAs

■ Deposits.

Most institutions allow unlimited deposits of any size to their MMDAs. There are exceptions, however. A number of institutions require that deposits be at least $100, and a few set the minimum even higher. The highest minimum deposit in our survey was $500 at First Texas in Dallas.

■ Withdrawals and Transfers.

You can gain access to the funds in your money market account in several different ways. Withdrawals can be made at teller windows or ATMs. Funds can also be transferred by third-party check, telephone transfer to another account, or preauthorized transfer to pay bills. Federal regulations limit these indirect transfers to six a month, with a maximum of three third-party checks included in that total.

Financial institutions differ widely in their policies on minimum transaction size and maximum number of all transactions. Most allow an unlimited number of deposits and direct withdrawals, and allow the legal limit on indirect transfers, with no minimum size, and charge no fees. This is the most favorable policy to savers, and you should seek it out.

Several institutions require a minimum size on direct withdrawals. The highest minimum we encountered was $500 at Baltimore Federal, Citibank in New York, and Continental Illinois in Chicago.

All the financial institutions we surveyed allowed some in-person withdrawals at no charge, as long as minimum balance requirements were met. However, Mercantile National Bank in Dallas charged $.25 for on-premise ATM withdrawals and the Bank of New England in Boston charged $.15 for all ATM transactions.

Several institutions limit the number of free withdrawals that can be made from MMDAs. First City in Houston charged $3 per withdrawal in excess of three per month; however, it exempted ATM transactions from this limit. Others had higher limits or lower fees.

Accounts that allow unlimited free withdrawals are preferable to those that do not. Since most savers make few withdrawals from MMDAs, restrictions on the number of withdrawals does not seriously limit the usefulness of these accounts.

Money Market Funds (MMFs)

Money market funds were first introduced in 1972, but became popular with consumers only in the late 1970s when interest rates soared. They invest in a variety of short-term securities that earn market rates of interest. After a portion of the earnings is retained as a management fee (generally between .5% and .75%), these earnings are credited to the shareholders.

The funds maintain the value of a share at $1, so that an MMF account works very much like a bank account: a purchase of 1000 shares costs $1000. Earnings are paid in shares, rather than allowing the value of a share to increase. So if you invested $1000 in a fund for one year, and earnings averaged 10%, at the end of the year you would own 1,100 shares worth $1,100.

MMFs work in very much the same way as MMDAs at banks. Deposits and withdrawals may be made at any time, and there are minimum transaction sizes, and minimum balance requirements.

■ Advantages and Disadvantages over MMDAs.

MMFs offer the following advantages over MMDAs:

You can open an account with an initial deposit of only $1000 and sometimes only $500, although there are some funds that require deposits of $50,000. On the other hand, many funds have lower minimums for IRA accounts.

Most funds charge no fees of any kind except for wire transfers and the built-in management fee. The major exceptions to this rule are funds that are part of cash management accounts (which carry annual fees of up to $100), and funds offered by some brokerage houses that levy a charge if your account does not generate a minimum amount in commissions for buying or selling securities.

Minimum balance requirements for keeping your account open are usually only $500, and as little as $1 at some funds. If your account does not meet the requirement, it is merely closed after sixty days and the balance is mailed to you. Your account continues to earn interest until it is closed.

MMFs have the following disadvantages compared with MMDAs:

They are not insured by an agency of the federal government. In fact, they are usually not insured at all, and are therefore riskier than accounts at federally insured banks, S & Ls, and credit unions.

They are not as accessible as accounts at local financial institutions. In order to withdraw money, you must make a phone call, write a check, or write a letter. You cannot go to a nearby ATM and withdraw cash.

They are more difficult to evaluate than accounts at financial institutions. You must not only compare yields and features, but also evaluate the risk of each fund you are considering. Funds that invest in short-term securities are safer than those investing in longer-term securities.

■ MMFs Available to General Public.

There are five types of money market funds available to the general public.

General-purpose funds.

These are the most common types of funds. They invest in a variety of money market instruments.

Government-only funds.
These invest only in securities issued by the federal government or its agencies. Government-only funds are somewhat safer than general-purpose funds. Most, however, invest in repurchase agreements that are backed by government securities, and are not as safe as the securities themselves.

Funds exempt from federal income tax.
These invest primarily in obligations of state and local governments that are exempt from federal income taxes. They are recommended for individuals in the 36% or higher income tax bracket.

Funds exempt from both federal taxes and income taxes in the state for which they were designed.
These invest primarily in municipal securities issued by governments within the state for which they were designed. They are suitable for individuals in a combined federal and state income tax bracket of over 40%.

Tied funds.
These are components of cash management accounts, or open only to customers of a particular brokerage firm. Tied funds are generally available in all of the first three forms above.

With the exception of the investments that they make and the customers they are designed for, all of the funds work in about the same way. In order to open an account, you must first request a prospectus, as required by federal security laws. You must then fill out a simple application form and either mail or wire a minimum initial investment to the fund.

■ Withdrawals.

There are several ways you can withdraw money. The easiest and most popular method is to write a check to either yourself or a third party. Almost all funds provide this service. Minimum check size ranges from no minimum (with CMA accounts) to $500. Most funds require a minimum check size of $500. A few non-CMA funds require only $250.

A second way to withdraw funds is through telephone transfer. Under this method, money is either transferred by wire to your checking account or mailed to you by check. Many funds charge a nominal wire-transfer fee, generally about $5. A third way to withdraw funds is by sending a "stock power" form to the fund, requesting a withdrawal. This method is generally used only to close an account. Finally, many funds have systematic withdrawal programs. Under this method a monthly or quarterly check of specified size will be mailed to you. Funds providing this service often require that you keep a minimum balance of $5000 or $10,000, and often require a minimum systematic withdrawal of at least $25. This method of withdrawal is especially good for IRA accounts in the withdrawal stage.

The following table gives details (including toll-free telephone numbers when available) for the largest money market funds. If you live in the same state as the fund's headquarters, the toll-free number will not work, and you should call them collect. The fund will send you a prospectus and an application form. To invest, complete and return the application form with your payment.

Table 1
LARGEST MONEY MARKET FUNDS

Name	*Type*	*Minimum Investment/ Initial Addition*	*Minimum Balance*	*Minimum Check*	*Systematic Withdrawal (Minimum Balance/ Check)*
Carnegie Liquid Capital Income Trust (800) 321-2322	Reg.	1000/250	500	500	No
Centennial Daily Cash Fund	Reg.	500/25		250	5000/40
(800) 525-7048	IRA	250/25		250	5000/40
Dean Witter Active Assets (800) 222-3326	CMA $50 yr. fee	20,000/none*		None	

Name	*Type*	*Minimum Investment/ Initial Addition*	*Minimum Balance*	*Minimum Check*	*Systematic Withdrawal (Minimum Balance/ Check)*
Delaware Cash Reserves (800) 523-4640	Reg.	1000/25	1000	500	5000/40
Dreyfus Liquid Assets (800) 223-0303	Reg.	2500/100		500	
EF Hutton Cash Reserve Manag. (800) 522-1882	CMA	10,000/1000**	500	500	No
Federated Tax Free Instruments Trust (800) 245-2423	Fed. Tax Free	500/100	500	100	No
Fidelity Cash Reserves (800) 544-6666	Reg.	1000/250	500	500	No
Fidelity Daily Income Trust (800) 544-6666	CMA	10,000/500	5000	None	No
Kemper Money Market Fund (800)621-1048	Reg.	1000/100		500	
Merrill Lynch CMA Money Fund (800) 221-4146	CMA	20,000/2500*		None	No
Merrill Lynch Ready Assets (800) 522-5560	Reg.	5000/1000	1000	500	—/50
Merrill Lynch Government Fund (800) 225-1576	Gov. only	5000/1000	1000	500	No
Nuveen Tax Free Reserves (800) 621-7210	Fed. Tax Free	1000/100	None	500	
Paine Webber CASHFUND (212) 437-5306	Reg. IRA	5000/500 1000	500	500	
Prudential-Bache MoneyMart Assets (800) 221-7984	Reg.	1000/100	500	500	

Table 1 continued
LARGEST MONEY MARKET FUNDS

Name	*Type*	*Minimum Investment/ Initial Addition*	*Minimum Balance*	*Minimum Check*	*Systematic Withdrawal (Minimum Balance/ Check)*
Reserve Fund (800)223-5547	Reg.	1000/500	500	500	5000/25
Shearson Daily Dividend (212) 577-5794	Tied	2500/1000	500	NA	No
Scudder Cash Investment Trust (800) 225-2470	Reg.	1000/None	500	500	10,000/—
T Rowe Price (800) 638-5660	Reg.	1000/100	500	500	5000/50
Vanguard Money Market Trust (800) 523-7025	Reg. or insured	1000/100	500	None	10,000/—
Webster Cash Reserve (212) 635-5055	Tied	1500/500	500	NA	No

* In any account
** $5 semiannual fee if account doesn't generate $100 in commissions

Evaluating the Risk of Money Market Funds

Although they are reasonably safe, MMFs are not insured by agencies of the federal government, and therefore do involve some risk. There are three types of risk that depositors in money market funds are exposed to: market, solvency, and default.

Market risk is the possibility that the securities in which a fund invests will fall in value. This would happen if interest rates rose. The funds protect themselves from this risk by maintaining investment portfolios that have very short average maturity lengths. Most funds have an average maturity of from thirty to sixty days. The average maturity length for any fund will fluctuate with the interest-rate forecasts that management makes. If management thinks rates are about to fall, it will generally lengthen the average maturity of the fund's portfolio. Conversely, if it thinks rates will rise, the average maturity length will be shortened. Usually, funds do not sell their securities; they wait for them to mature.

A fund may experience a sudden run by its depositors and be unable to pay everybody on demand. This is *solvency risk*. The shorter the maturity length of a fund's portfolio, the lower the solvency risk. Funds have two other protections against insolvency. First, they can legally make their shareholders wait for up to seven days for payment. Second, funds are allowed to borrow against their assets.

Risk of default is the possibility that one of the issuers of an obligation that a fund holds will not repay its debt. To protect against this, funds invest only in very high-grade debt instruments. Nevertheless, some funds make investments that are riskier than others in order to realize a higher yield. The most common investments made by funds are listed below.

Treasury securities.

These are obligations of the U.S. Treasury. They are backed by the full faith and credit of the federal government, and are absolutely free of risk of default, but they are the lowest-yielding assets held by funds.

Agency securities.

These are obligations of agencies of the U.S. government, such as the Small Business Administration. Many of these securities are only moral obligations of the federal government, and are not backed by its full faith and credit. While it is very unlikely that Congress would ever allow a government agency to default on its obligations, delays are possible. These securities yield about .5% more than Treasury securities.

Domestic bank CDs.

Only the first $100,000 of each of these CDs are insured. Since they are often issued in denominations of tens of millions of dollars, they involve some risk of default. Funds generally limit themselves to purchasing CDs from major commercial banks and S & Ls. Since federal regulators have shown that they are loath to allow a major financial institution to collapse, these investments are quite safe. Further, funds monitor the financial health of these institutions closely. For example, the funds liquidated their positions in Continental Illinois CDs at least six months prior to that bank's near collapse. Domestic bank CDs pay about .75% more than Treasury securities.

Bankers acceptances.
These instruments are similar to a postdated check that is authorized (accepted) by a major commercial bank. Bankers acceptances are used primarily in international trade. Those issued by U.S. banks have about the same risk and offer the same yield as domestic CDs.

Letters of credit.
Similar to bankers acceptances, these instruments authorize a foreign correspondent of a U.S. bank to pay the holder funds. They have about the same risk and yield as bankers acceptances.

Eurodollar CDs.
These are obligations of foreign branches of U.S. banks that are denominated in dollars. These CDs expose funds to political risk. For example, a country could impose currency controls, making it impossible for the foreign branch to pay its obligations. These are riskier but yield about .50% more than domestic bank CDs.

Yankee CDs.
These are issued by the U.S. branches of foreign banks. They have about the same risk and yield as Eurodollar CDs.

Commercial paper.
These are the short-term, unsecured debts of major domestic corporations. The best commercial paper is rated A-1 by Standard and Poors, and P-1 by Moody's. The lowest-rated paper any fund will invest in is rated A-3 or P-3, which means that the rating services think the issuer has only a satisfactory capacity for timely repayment.

Most funds will not buy commercial paper rated lower than A-2 or P-2. The highest-rated commercial paper has about the same yield as domestic bank CDs. A-3 and P-3 paper yields about 1% more than A-1 and P-1 paper.

Repurchase agreements (Repos).

Under these arrangements, funds buy securities, usually Treasury securities, with an agreement that the original owner will buy them back at a given time, usually the next day, at an agreed-upon price. The difference between the two prices represents the interest the fund earns on the arrangement.

Since the securities involved may never leave the possession of the original owner, repos can be construed as a secured loan rather than an outright sale. If the issuer goes bankrupt while the repo is in force, the fund will have to wait in line with other creditors to recover the securities. Consequently, repos are not as safe as the securities that underlie them.

Some government-only funds invest heavily in repos. In fact, the Reserve Fund's government-only money market fund was 100% invested in repos at the time its last annual report was issued.

Municipals.

These are generally the obligations of state and local governments. Only tax-exempt funds invest in them. Municipals are also rated by the services, with the highest-quality issues rated AAA and Aaa. The lowest-grade municipal most funds will invest in is rated AA or Aa.

Choosing a Money Market Fund

When choosing a money market fund, you should consider the yield it offers, the convenience of its special features (such as minimum deposits), and the risk you are willing to take. The first step is to obtain prospectuses and annual reports from each fund you are considering, and evaluate them carefully. Then compare annual yields over several years of a number of funds. This information is usually contained in the annual reports and publications of various reporting services available in many libraries.

Two publications, though expensive, may help you decide on an MMF. They are *Donoghue's Moneyletter*, and the Institute for Econometric Research's *Money Fund Safety Ratings. Donoghue's* gives complete information on all MMFs. *Money Fund Safety Ratings* rates funds on a scale of A to D. It also identifies funds that, in its opinion, offer the best yields for a given level of risk.

Table 2 gives the yields of the large funds listed in Table 1. Table 3 gives investments.

Table 2
YIELDS OF LARGE FUNDS

Name	*6/83–6/84*	*6/84–6/85*
Centennial	9.1%	8.7%
Dean Witter	9.1	9.4
Delaware Cash	9.1	9.2
Dreyfus Liquid	9.1	9.3
E. F. Hutton	9.4	9.4
Fidelity Cash	9.1	9.0
Fidelity Daily	9.3	9.0
Kemper Money	9.5	9.4
Merrill CMA	9.1	9.3
Merrill Ready	9.0	9.4
Nuveen Tax Free	4.8	NA
Paine Webber	9.1	9.1
Prudential	9.4	9.3
Reserve Fund	8.9	8.9
Shearson Daily	9.2	9.0
Scudder	8.8	8.9
T Rowe Price	9.3	9.3
Webster	9.1	9.1

Source: *Forbes*

Table 3
INVESTMENTS OF FUNDS

The numbers listed across the top of this table correspond with the investments listed beneath the table. The numbers listed vertically under column 8 indicate the lowest-grade commercial paper in which the corresponding fund will invest (2 represents A2, P2 paper). The letters in column 10 indicate the lowest-grade municipals in which a fund will invest.

Fund	*1*	*2*	*3*	*4*	*5*	*6*	*7*	*8*	*9*	*10*
Carnegie	x	x	x	x	x		x	2	x	
Centennial	x	x	x	x	x	x		1	x	
Dean Witter	x	x	x	x				2	x	
Delaware	x	x	x	x	x	x	x	2	x	
Dreyfus Liq.	x	x	x	x		x		1	x	
E. F. Hutton	x	x	x	x		x	x	1	x	
Federated										AA
Fidelity Cash	x	x	x	x		x	x	1	x	
Fidelity Daily	x	x	x	x	x			1	x	
Kemper	x	x	x	x		x	x	2	x	
Merrill CMA	x	x	x	x	x	x		3	x	
Merril Ready	x	x	x	x	x	x		3	x	
Merrill Govt.	x	x							x	
Nuveen Tax Free										AA
Paine Webber	x	x	x	x				1	x	
Prudential	x	x	x	x		x	x	1	x	
Reserve Fund	x	x	x	x	x	x			x	
Shearson	x	x	x	x		x	x	1	x	
Scudder	x	x	x	x		x		1	x	
T Rowe Price	x	x	x	x		x	x	2	x	
Vanguard	x	x	x	x				1	x	
Webster	x	x	x	x		x	x	1	x	

Investments: 1. Treasury securities; 2. Agency securities; 3. Domestic bank CDs; 4. Bankers acceptances; 5. Letters of credit; 6. Eurodollar CDs; 7. Yankee CDs; 8. Commercial paper; 9. Repurchase agreements; 10. Municipals

CHECKLIST

Use this checklist when shopping for MMDAs.

Minimum opening balance ________

Minimum balance to earn high interest ________

How is balance computed? ________

Method of computing interest ________

Average yield last year ________

Current yield ________

Is rate paid tied to an index? ________

Minimum deposit ________

Minimum check ________

Minimum withdrawal ________

Maximum number of withdrawals

- By check ________
- By transfer ________
- Direct ________

Service charges

- Account maintenance fee ________
- Minimum balance to avoid fee ________
- How computed ________
- Regular transaction fees
  - Direct ________
  - By check or transfer ________

C H E C K L I S T

Use this checklist when shopping for MMFs.

Minimum initial investment ____________

Minimum additional investment ____________

Minimum check size ____________

Minimum balance ____________

Average yield last year ____________

Most recent yield ____________

Investments authorized by prospectus ____________

Other services available ____________

Fees ____________

  Excess transaction fees

    Direct ____________

    By check or transfer ____________

  Other fees (e.g., balance inquiry) ____________

7

Investment Options

RECOMMENDATIONS

Investment options such as stocks and bonds represent an alternative to savings accounts for some consumers. These investments may pay higher yields than savings options, yet they entail greater risk. You should not invest in them unless you have at least three months' income in liquid savings (e.g., money market deposit account or passbook savings account); you have adequate life, health, and disability insurance; and you are prepared to assume fairly high risks.

Stocks are generally preferable to bonds. Stock investors usually are paid dividends and, if the price of shares rises, earn capital gains as well. Bonds, on the other hand, have performed more poorly than some safer, more liquid investment options like Treasury bills.

Over the long run, the only way to achieve better-than-average investment results is to assume an above-average level

continued on next page

continued

of risk. Almost always, for example, stocks with the highest dividends are those whose prices are most likely to remain unchanged or decline.

There are two strategies for minimizing the risk of stock investments. One is to diversify your stock portfolio by investing in a number of different stocks unrelated to each other. If you decide to do so, be prepared to spend much time studying the fundamentals of investment and evaluating specific securities.

An easier strategy is to invest in a mutual fund. When selecting such a fund, be aware that a fund's previous performance is not a good predictor of its future performance. A fund that did very well last year, or even over the past five or ten years, is just as likely to underperform in the market this year as a fund with a poor track record. To a very large extent, fund performance is random.

Yet there is one kind of mutual fund that is likely to do worse than others. This is a specialty fund, which invests in only one type of security—for example, gold-mining stocks. We recommend avoiding them.

One of the best ways to minimize risk in the stock market is to invest in an index fund. These funds maintain a securities portfolio that mirrors a broad market average, such as the Standard and Poor 500. But even an index fund will not protect you if the market as a whole declines substantially.

No matter what kind of fund you choose, select one with no or low commission fees (no-load funds).

Stocks

In the past forty years, stock investors as a whole have earned much better than average rates of return. However, these yields have fluctuated greatly. During the 1970s, for example, stocks were among the least profitable investments available. This variability in the rate of return is the risk involved in stock market investments.

Consumers considering purchasing stocks should first take the time to read a good book on investment. One of the best and easiest to read is *A Random Walk Down Wall Street* (Norton, 1985), by Burton Malkiel. If you do not have the patience to study such a primer, you should not be investing in the stock market; you would be better off with one of the savings options discussed earlier in this book.

Economists and other experts have been studying the stock market for decades. They agree on a number of points:

- The stock market is efficient. This means that the current price of any security reflects fully the market's best estimate of the future prospects for the company that those shares represent. In other words, the small investor should not think he can "beat the market." More often, the market beats him.
- There is no theory or system that can be shown to outperform the market consistently over the long run. Any system might outperform the market for a year, or even a decade. But over the long run, no particular system has been shown to be superior to selecting a portfolio randomly.
- It is impossible to call turns in the market. The market has no memory. Security prices are a random walk.
- The market does not reward investors for accepting nonsystematic risks (those that can be reduced by diversified stock investments).

There are two types of risk in stock investment: systematic and nonsystematic. Systematic risk is related to the broad movements of the market as a whole, and cannot be reduced by diversifying your stock portfolio. Nonsystematic risk relates to the risk of a particular security, and can be reduced or eliminated through diversification.

When choosing a diversified portfolio of stocks, make sure that your securities are not closely related. For example, if you buy stock in Sears and stock in Whirlpool, Sears's major appliance supplier, you will not significantly reduce risk. When Sears's business is bad, Whirlpool is likely to be doing poorly as well.

There are a few rules that should be followed by stock market investors. Although these rules will not guarantee good investment results, they will at least prevent you from making disastrous mistakes.

1. Before buying a stock, investigate the company fully. Read all the information you can get about it, including its annual reports and any research reports. Make sure that its price is fully justified by its balance sheet and future prospects.

2. Avoid stocks that are the current glamour issues on the street. They are likely to be overpriced, and it is almost certain that their bubble will eventually burst.

3. Invest only in stocks that you believe have good prospects for sustained long-term growth.

4. Take full advantage of favorable tax laws. Sell losing stocks before they turn into long-term capital losses. Hold on to stocks with gains as long as is possible and prudent. There are two benefits from holding on to winners. Long-term capital gains are taxed at favorable rates, and no tax liability is incurred until the stock is actually sold and the gain is realized.

5. Stay abreast of developments in the securities you own. A stock market portfolio does not thrive on neglect.

Mutual Funds

If you lack the temperament, fortitude, and time necessary for successful stock market investment, you can invest in a mutual fund, which pools the money of many investors to purchase a variety of securities. This way you can rely on experts and diversify your portfolio even when you invest only small sums of money.

Mutual funds offer three principal advantages over making your own investment decisions. They allow diversification. You can make small, regular investments without incurring the high commission costs associated with buying small lots of securities. And mutual funds do not require your constant attention.

Mutual fund salespeople also claim that the professional management of a fund is of great advantage to small investors. However, there is no convincing evidence that the professional managers of funds do any better than a randomly selected portfolio of securities would. Yet you must try to assess the competence of a fund's managers before you invest, because incompetent managers can do substantially worse than a randomly selected portfolio.

There are several different types of mutual funds from which you can choose.

■ Closed-End Funds.

After the initial shares are sold, no further investments into these funds are accepted. Shares of a closed-end fund are traded like stocks. Typically, these funds sell at a discount from net asset value (the market value of all securities in the fund's portfolio, divided by the number of shares outstanding), although a few such funds often sell at premiums over net asset value. Closed-end funds are especially attractive when they are selling at large discounts. Before buying, be sure you know what the typical discount is.

■ Open-End Funds.

Additional shares of these funds are issued on a continuous basis, with the proceeds going into the fund's investment portfolio. Occasionally, open-end funds will temporarily be closed to new investors. Most funds are of this type.

■ Load Funds.

These funds charge a commission of up to 8.5% to purchase shares. The commission goes to pay salesmen. There are no advantages to load funds. Avoid them.

■ No-Load Funds.

These funds charge no commission. They should be considered.

■ Specialty Funds.

These funds invest in only one type of security. You should avoid them unless you are prepared to accept fairly high risks.

■ Index Funds.

These funds invest in a wide range of securities. Portfolios are constructed to mirror movements in a broad market index, usually the Standard and Poor 500.

In addition to the above, most mutual fund companies offer funds designed with specific investment objectives—for example, capital gains, speculative growth, or dividends.

Most consumers would be best off with a no-load index fund. These funds assure you that your stocks do about as well as the market in general. The only limitation of these funds is that they do not hold foreign securities or stocks not traded on major exchanges. If you decide to buy another type of fund, look for one that appears to follow the investment rules explained earlier in this chapter, and avoid those that have high loads.

Bonds

Bond markets are complex and confusing. Over the past thirty-five years, corporate bonds have underperformed short-term savings options such as Treasury securities. Yet they have subjected their owners to a substantial amount of risk.

As a rule, the longer the maturity of a bond, the higher its yield. This holds in all but the most unusual circumstances. However, the longer the maturity, the higher the risk as well.

The problem with long-term bonds is that they lock you into a fixed rate of interest for as long as thirty years. If interest rates rise, the price of long-term bonds falls precipitously. Of course, a decline in interest rates causes the value of long-term bonds to rise. Moreover, the potential for capital gains is often limited by call provisions. These provisions allow companies to recall their bonds, and redeem them at face value. If interest rates should fall by more than 2% or 3%, most companies will exercise their call provisions.

In addition to market risk, corporate bonds also subject their owners to risk of default. Although rating services evaluate the creditworthiness of the companies that issue the bonds, they cannot see twenty or thirty years into the future. Remember that many of the railroads that went bankrupt in the 1960s once enjoyed the very highest credit ratings.

If you are considering investing in bonds, you would be best off investing in a bond fund. They are much more liquid than bonds themselves, and offer the advantage of diversification.

Choosing a Broker

If you want to invest in the stock market or purchase shares in a closed-end mutual fund, you will require the services of a stockbroker. There are currently three types of brokerage firms from which to choose.

■ Full-Service Firms.

These have research departments, offer advice on which securities to buy and when to sell, and carry a full range of investment products. They charge the highest commissions for transactions. When dealing with a full-service broker, you will receive the personal attention of an account executive.

If you want the research reports generated by brokerage houses, or need somebody to hold your hand when your portfolio is performing badly, you will find the extra service of a full-service firm worth the additional cost. If you choose to deal with such a firm, select one that has a large research department.

■ Discount Brokerage Firms.

These offer cut-rate prices, but very little service beyond order taking. If you feel comfortable making your trading decisions without outside advice, and don't desire the personal attention of an account executive, you will save a substantial amount of money by using a discount broker.

■ Bank Brokerage Services.

Brokerage services provided by banks range from full service to bare-bones discount. The services are actually provided by firms to whom the bank leases desk space, since a federal regulation prohibits banks from giving investment advice except through their trust departments. Fees charged by banks are comparable to those charged by other firms for the same level of service.

The advantage of a bank-provided service is that your investment account can be tied into a bank asset-management account. These asset-management accounts are similar to the cash management accounts offered by brokerage houses (see Chapter 3). They are usually cheaper than the accounts offered by brokerage houses, and generally require smaller total balances.

Trust Departments

Most major banks, and many smaller ones, have trust departments whose primary business is to set up and administer trusts. The departments are often headed by an attorney, and always have a legal staff.

Trusts can be set up in many different forms, with many different investment objectives and instructions. Trust departments are usually equipped to deal with any permutation possible. In all cases, there is a fee for every service provided.

Many customers of trust departments allow them to make investment decisions. Unless the trust is quite large, generally over $1 million, the bank will simply invest the funds in a house mutual fund. Larger trusts get the personal attention of a trust officer, who personally directs investment of the funds in the trust. However, the officer is subject to the investment policy of the bank and restricted to approved securities.

The trust department will carry out all the provisions of the trust agreement, and administer wills. This includes such mundane tasks as bill paying or selling assets of an estate. As always, there are fees for these services. In general, a fee structure is agreed upon at the time a trust is placed with the bank.

Trust departments also provide custodial services. Under this type of arrangement, the bank simply houses securities, and the customer directs trades. The department may use its own in-house brokerage services, or may use the services of an outside brokerage firm. In either case, there will be a fee for housing the account, and probably an additional fee for each transaction. Most people would be better off with an account at a full-service broker.

Trust departments sometimes accept walk-in purchases from a noncustomer. Under this arrangement, the trust department buys securities for the individual. The charges for such services are much higher than those incurred at full-service brokerage houses, and consumers should not use trust departments in this capacity. Further, many of these transactions involve government securities which can be purchased directly from the government at no cost (see Chapter 3).

8

Installment Loans

RECOMMENDATIONS

Before you decide to take out an installment loan, consider paying with cash, even if you must defer the purchase until sufficient funds are saved. Paying with cash is usually cheaper than obtaining financing from a lending institution, if the funds that would be used for monthly installments are deposited in some type of savings account, and if inflation rates are well below loan rates.

If it is necessary to borrow, shop carefully for credit, remembering that costs vary greatly. First, explore the possibility of borrowing from parents or other family members at a low rate. If this is not possible, try to borrow from an insurance company on a whole-life policy, from a credit union, or from a bank, using a CD as security. If at all possible, do not borrow from finance companies.

continued on next page

continued

Second, do not purchase insurance offered by the lender—credit life or accident and health—unless there is no other way to protect yourself and your family against default due to illness or death.

When to Borrow

Many families mistakenly take out installment loans when they do not need them or cannot afford them. Before deciding whether to borrow money, ask yourself the following three questions.

■ Do I Need Credit?

Consumers often borrow in two situations in which credit should be avoided. The first is when they do not need or really want a product whose purchase must be financed. Easy access to installment loans may encourage you to make expensive purchases you later regret. The solution to this problem is simple: If you are considering a specific product, resist any sales pressure to buy immediately. Instead, take a day to think it over.

The second situation is when you can afford to pay cash. Paying cash is almost always cheaper than using credit, as the following example suggests. A $4000 used car financed over a four-year period at 15% will cost approximately $1200 in finance charges. Yet if you withdraw this $4000 from a money market account paying 7%, then deposit the equivalent of monthly payments back into the account, you lose only $500 interest. Thus, paying cash would cost about $700 less than borrowing. Of course, this savings will vary depending on factors such as the loan rate, savings yield, inflation rates, and your willingness to replenish the savings after you have withdrawn them to make a purchase. It will also depend on the proportion of interest payments that are tax-deductible.

■ Can I Afford Credit?

Before borrowing, ask whether you can meet all essential expenses and still afford monthly loan payments. You can make this calculation in two ways. One is to add up all basic monthly expenses and compare this total with your take-home pay. If the difference would not cover a monthly payment and still leave funds for less regular expenses, you cannot afford the loan. For example, assume a family with $2000 in monthly take-home pay and other income has monthly expenses for food, rent, utilities, and insurance totaling approximately $1500. There is no way this family can afford $350 monthly payments and still cover other expenses such as clothing, personal-care products, and emergencies.

An even more reliable method is to ask if you currently save enough of your take-home pay to afford the monthly payments. If you do not, it probably will be difficult to forgo other purchases in order to make the payments. Are you prepared to give up spending on clothing, entertainment, or eating out in order to afford the new car or home improvements you wish to finance? Remember that once you have taken out an installment loan there is usually a substantial cost in getting rid of it. It almost always requires giving up the product that was financed.

One rule of thumb financial advisers suggest is to limit consumer debt to one-fifth of after-tax income. For example, a family with an after-tax income of $20,000 should never owe more than $4000 in installment and credit card debt.

■ Can I Qualify for Credit?

The irony of borrowing is that the more you need credit, the more difficult it is to obtain and the more it costs. Lenders talk about evaluating the "capacity," "character," and "collateral" of a loan applicant: Can you repay the debt? Will you repay the debt? Is the lender fully protected if you fail to repay? Specifically, lenders place most importance on the following factors:

Your credit record.

Have you ever borrowed money? Have you paid loans off promptly?

Your income.

Will your income allow you to cover basic expenses and still make loan payments? Does your employment record suggest you will continue to receive this income?

Your net assets.

Do you possess savings or other assets that can be used to repay the loan if you lose your job? Do you have other debts that would have first claim on these assets?

The product financed.

Typically, the product being financed "secures" the loan. In the event of default, the lender may repossess it without even going to court. Consequently, it is easier to obtain a loan for a car than for home improvements, for instance. This is why lenders are least willing to extend credit that is "unsecured" by a specific product or other asset.

Because they do not have a credit record, those who have never borrowed are at a disadvantage in obtaining credit. To establish such a record, open a charge account with a department store, making certain to pay bills promptly. Or establish a savings account at a bank or credit union, then borrow on these funds. Sometimes those without a credit record who have satisfactorily maintained a checking account can secure an installment loan at the same institution.

The only factor a creditor can consider in deciding whether to give you a loan is your creditworthiness—whether it appears you will be able to pay off the loan. The Equal Credit Opportunity Act prohibits lenders from discriminating against you on the basis of race, age, sex, marital status, or receipt of public assistance. Moreover, if a lender denies you credit, he or she must notify you within thirty days of the completion of your application, and either explain the specific reasons for this refusal or indicate your right to an explanation.

If a lender informs you that information in your credit record suggests you are a poor credit risk, you have the right to check this record and request that it be corrected. The records are kept by local credit bureaus. The Fair Credit Reporting Act requires that, on request, credit bureaus provide you a summary of your file and investigate any errors you report. If you disagree with the results of this investigation, you have the right to add your own statement to the file, which the credit bureau must include in future reports to creditors

Where to Borrow

In seeking an installment loan, most consumers think first of borrowing from a bank or finance company. There are, however, other credit sources, and some of these are less expensive.

■ Family.

Parents or other family members are sometimes willing to lend funds at low rates. They may charge you only the interest they would have earned on the money—the 5½% earned on a passbook account, or the 7% to 8% earned on a money market deposit account or money market fund account. In addition, they are likely to treat you relatively leniently in the event unforeseen circumstances cause delinquency or default.

■ Life Insurance Companies.

Most consumers with whole-life insurance policies can borrow on the accumulated cash value of the policy at a guaranteed rate. This rate is often less than rates charged by commercial banks. But keep in mind that borrowing this cash value reduces your insurance policy's financial protection unless you purchase term insurance to make up the difference. This term insurance, however, is usually available only to those with policies that pay dividends ("participating" policies).

■ Credit Unions.

Credit unions are nonprofit consumer cooperatives that were first organized to provide members loans with lower rates and more sympathetic terms than those offered by profit-making institutions. Today, credit union loan rates approximate those charged by commercial banks. But these coops frequently provide free credit life insurance and they are often willing to make small loans to customers in need. They tend to be lenient to borrowers with legitimate payment problems, and they sometimes pay dividends in the form of interest rebates at the end of the fiscal year.

The principal limitation of credit unions is that they are not available to everyone. Most are associated with an employer or a trade union; only employees or members can join. But there are also credit unions associated with churches, communities, and other groups. We urge you to explore their availability.

■ Commercial Banks.

Most consumer installment loans are purchased at commercial banks. Rates typically range from 10% to 20%, depending on factors explained in the next section. One point to remember: the more secure the loan's collateral, the lower the rate. Thus, borrowing on a CD held at a specific bank is usually the cheapest way to borrow at that institution.

■ Finance Companies.

Finance companies often lend to those who cannot obtain credit from banks or credit unions. Because their bad-debt losses and their own borrowing costs are higher, they usually charge higher rates. Typically, these rates range from 15% to 30%. If you are denied credit by a bank or credit union, you should question your ability to afford the higher rate of a loan company.

■ Automobile Finance Companies.

The only finance companies that often charge lower rates than commercial banks are those affiliated with major automobile manufacturers—General Motors Acceptance Corporation, Ford Motor Credit, and other companies. Recently, in an effort to promote the sale of cars, these companies have been offering low rates on certain models. But keep in mind that a car dealer offering you such a rate may be less willing to discount the price of the car or throw in free options. A dealer's unwillingness to "sweeten the deal" may cost you more than any saving from the lower interest rates. To avoid this, negotiate a purchase price before informing the dealer you need financing.

■ Retailers.

Many car dealers write installment contracts, then sell them to banks or finance companies. These loans are essentially bank or finance-company loans. Most of the credit offered and serviced by retailers, however, is "open-end" through charge cards, which are discussed in the next chapter.

Yet a few retailers write and "carry" their own installment loans. Typically, these merchants are used-car lots or furniture and appliance stores selling to moderate-income families. The reasons these loans are serviced by retailers vary greatly, but often include the inability to sell risky installment notes to financial institutions, the desire to build a customer relationship to sell additional merchandise, and the ability to profit from the lending. The latter is often possible because their loan rates are usually higher than those charged by most other credit sources, and are generally similar to those offered by finance companies.

Loan Rates

Loan rates are influenced principally by four factors: the size of the loan, its security or collateral, the type of lending institution, and the specific lending institution.

■ Size of Loan.

Generally speaking, the larger the loan, the lower the rate. In many states, these differences reflect progressively lower ceilings established by law. Thus, in several states a finance company can charge more than 30% on loans under $500, up to 30% on loans between $500 and $1000, but only up to 20% on loans over several thousand dollars.

■ Security.

The quality of the security or collateral that protects a lender's interest also influences the loan rate. The greater the likelihood that the security can be used, in the event of default, to recover what was lent, the higher its quality and the lower the loan rate.

The highest-quality securities are assets controlled by the lending institution, such as the cash value of a whole-life insurance policy or a CD. In case of default, the lender can take these assets to recover the loan principal and related expenses.

Also of relatively high quality is home equity when the lending institution is also the mortgagor. Recently, many banks have offered mortgagees the opportunity to borrow on their home equity at relatively low rates. In a default, these institutions have the ability to foreclose on a home. The principal danger with these loans is that credit limits are usually so high that families may increase their debt well beyond prudent levels. In doing so, they may substantially reduce their home equity, the principal savings for many households.

The most common security is the product that is financed. For most auto loans, the car itself is the collateral. This is also usually true of furniture or appliance loans. Because these products can depreciate rapidly in value, the quality of this security is lower than that of collateral held by lenders.

Other factors being equal, loans with the highest rates are those which are unsecured, that is, not guaranteed by a specific asset. But this does not mean that in a default, lenders are defenseless. As explained in the final section of this chapter, by going to court they can attach other assets—funds in a checking or savings account, for example.

■ Type of Lending Institution.

In the previous seciton it was noted that some lending institutions charge higher rates than others. These differences are illustrated below, showing the typical range of new-car loan rates at major lending institutions in mid-1985.

Banks	11–16%
Credit unions	10–15
Finance companies	15–20
Auto finance companies	10–14

■ Specific Lending Institution.

Among any given type of lending institutions in an area, loan rates tend to cluster. Yet there is usually a spread of at least two percentage points between the highest and lowest rates offered by banks or finance companies. In some areas, this spread is as high as four or five percentage points. Although this may not seem like much, just a two-percentage-point difference can mean considerable extra cost or saving. On a four-year $8000 loan, the difference represents more than $300. With a four-percentage-point spread, the difference exceeds $600.

The Federal Reserve Board periodically collects information on consumer loan rates from its member banks. These data provide valuable information about the average level, range, and regional variation of loan rates. They also suggest how rates vary depending on the type of security.

According to the FRB data, in August 1985 there was $512 billion in outstanding installment credit; 47% of this was held by commercial banks, 21% by finance companies, 15% by credit unions, and the remainder by other lending institutions. The FRB questioned member banks about rates for three types of installment credit: a forty-eight-month new-car loan, a twenty-four-month personal loan, and a 120-month mobile home loan. Their responses are summarized below.

New car loan rates.

New car loan rates ranged from a low of 9.8% (First of America Bank in Detroit) to a high of 16.3% (First Interstate Bank of Arizona), with an average of 12.7%. Almost all big money-center banks that reported (not all did) charged rates above the average: For example, Chase Manhattan charged 15.3%, Manufacturers Hanover 15.0%, Chemical 13.8%, and Bank of America 13.8%. In addition, rates tended to cluster in metropolitan areas. An example of clustering within an area is the range of rates from 13.5% to 14.0% at the four reporting San Francisco banks.

These data can be misleading, however, because of the small sample of institutions supplying information. A San Francisco Consumer Action new car loan survey in 1984 revealed a range of 3.6 percentage points on an $8000 forty-eight-month loan.

Table 1
NEW CAR LOAN RATES AT CALIFORNIA BANKS (1984)

Institution	*Fixed APR*	*Institution*	*Fixed APR*
Mitsubishi Bank	13.40	National American Bank	14.50
First National Bank	13.75	Sears Savings Bank	14.50
Golden State Sanwa Bank	13.75	United Bank	14.50
Bankcal	14.00	Bank of the Orient	14.75
World Savings & Loan	14.15	Gibraltar S & L	15.00
Bank of the West	14.25	Union Bank	15.00
California Federal S & L	14.25	California National Bank	15.25
Eureka Federal S & L	14.25	Mission National Bank	15.25
Hibernia Bank	14.25	Imperial Bank	15.47
Imperial S & L	14.25	American Asian Bank	15.50
S. F. Federal S & L	14.25	Redwood Bank	15.50
Sumitomo Bank	14.25	Alameda First Bank	15.75
		First Interstate Bank	15.75

Institution	Fixed APR	Institution	Fixed APR
Lloyds Bank	14.45	Atlas Savings & Loan	16.00
Bank of Canton	14.50	Wells Fargo Bank	16.00
Barclays Bank	14.50	Security Pacific Bank	16.11
Bay View Fed. S & L	14.50	Bank of America	16.75
California First Bank	14.50	Crocker Bank	17.00
First Enterprise Bank	14.50		
Mechanics Bank	14.50		

Personal loan rates.

Unsecured personal loan rates ranged from 11.8% (First National Bank and Trust in Tulsa) to 21% (United Bank in Denver and Fleet National Bank in Providence), with an average of 15.8%. Again, most reporting money-center banks charged above the average (Bank of America 19.5%, Chase Manhattan 17.0%, and Chemical 16.0%). Also, rates of reporting banks were closely clustered in cities like San Francisco, Atlanta, Detroit, and Columbus, Ohio.

Mobile-home loan rates.

Mobile-home rates ranged from 10.4% (National Bank of Alaska) to 17.5% (Huntington National in Columbus), with an average of 14.7%. Most banks surveyed, however, did not report rates for these loans.

Table 2 lists the rates reported by banks that responded to the Federal Reserve survey.

Table 2
*CONSUMER LOAN RATES (AUGUST 1985)**

State	*City*	*Bank*	*48-Mo. New Car*	*120-Mo. Mobile Home*	*24-Mo. Personal*
AL	Birmingham	AmSouth Bank	NA	NA	14.5%
AK	Anchorage	National Bank of Alaska	15.0%	10.4%	17.5
AZ	Phoenix	First Interstate Bank of Arizona	16.3	16.3	16.8

Table 2 continued
*CONSUMER LOAN RATES (AUGUST 1985)**

State	*City*	*Bank*	*48-Mo. New Car*	*120-Mo. Mobile Home*	*24-Mo. Personal*
AR	Little Rock	Worthen Bank & Trust Co.	12.5	14.5	12.5
CA	Los Angeles	First Interstate Bank of California	13.8	14.0	19.3
		Union Bank	12.5	NA	NA
	San Francisco	Bank of America	13.8	13.5	19.5
		Bank of California	13.5	15.0	19.0
		Crocker National Bank	14.0	NA	20.0
		Wells Fargo Bank	13.8	NA	19.5
CO	Denver	First Interstate Bank	14.5	NA	16.8
		United Bank	13.0	NA	21.0
CT	Hartford	Conn. Bank and Trust Co.	12.5	13.8	14.0
	New Britain	National Bank	13.5	14.0	16.0
DC	Washington	Riggs National Bank	12.0	NA	16.0
		Security National Bank	12.0	NA	15.0
FL	Fort Myers	First National Bank	14.9	NA	17.8
	Hialeah	Consolidated Bank	12.5	NA	18.0
	Miami	Southeast Bank	12.3	14.8	16.0
	Orlando	Barnett Bank of Central Florida	14.1	14.8	18.1

State	City	Bank	48-Mo. New Car	120-Mo. Mobile Home	24-Mo. Personal
	Stuart	First National Bank & Trust Co.	11.9	14.0	16.0
	Tampa	First National Bank of Florida	12.5	NA	15.9
GA	Atlanta	First National Bank	13.0	NA	13.0
		National Bank of Georgia	10.9	NA	13.0
		Trust Co. Bank	13.5	NA	14.0
	Augusta	Georgia Railroad Bank & Trust Co.	13.0	NA	15.0
	Macon	Trust Co. Bank of Middle Georgia	13.5	NA	15.5
IL	Aurora	National Bank	12.3	NA	19.0
	Chicago	Continental Illinois	13.0	NA	12.8
		First National Bank	12.3	15.3	17.8
		Harris Trust & Savings	12.5	NA	18.0
		La Salle National Bank	13.0	NA	17.8
		Merchandise National	14.5	NA	14.5
		Northern Trust Co.	12.3	NA	13.5
	Peoria	First National Bank	11.4	NA	16.4
IN	Evansville	Citizens National Bank	12.8	NA	14.0

Table 2 continued
*CONSUMER LOAN RATES (AUGUST 1985)**

State	*City*	*Bank*	*48-Mo. New Car*	*120-Mo. Mobile Home*	*24-Mo. Personal*
	Fort Wayne	Lincoln National Bank & Trust Co.	12.3	16.0	14.0
	Indianapolis	American Fletcher National Bank	13.3	NA	19.0
		Indiana National Bank	12.5	NA	20.0
		Merchants National Bank & Trust Co.	11.0	13.8	14.0
IA	Des Moines	Norwest Bank	12.8	NA	12.5
	Sioux City	Security National Bank	11.9	NA	16.4
KS	Topeka	First National Bank	12.8	13.5	16.0
KY	Louisville	Citizens Fidelity Bank & Trust Co.	13.5	NA	16.5
		First National Bank	13.5	NA	14.9
LA	Lafayette	First National Bank	13.0	14.5	18.0
MD	Baltimore	First National Bank of Maryland	13.5	16.0	18.0
		Maryland National Bank	13.5	14.5	17.9
		Union Trust Co. of Md.	12.5	14.5	16.5
MA	Andover	Baybank Merrimack Valley	13.5	NA	19.0

State	City	Bank	48-Mo. New Car	120-Mo. Mobile Home	24-Mo. Personal
	Boston	Bank of New England	13.5	NA	16.0
		First National Bank	12.5	NA	18.0
		Shawmut Bank	12.5	NA	16.0
		State Street Bank & Trust Co.	13.0	NA	16.5
	Worcester	Shawmut Worcester City Bank	12.5	NA	20.0
MI	Detroit	Comerica Bank	11.9	NA	15.5
		First of America Bank	9.8	15.0	15.0
		Manufacturers National	10.3	NA	14.3
		National Bank	9.9	NA	14.3
	Grand Rapids	Old Kent Bank and Trust Co.	11.5	NA	14.0
	Lansing	Michigan National Bank	11.0	NA	14.0
	Marquette	First National Bank & Trust Co.	11.9	15.0	15.0
	Mount Clemens	First National Bank in Mt. Clemens	13.0	15.0	15.0
	Pontiac	Community National Bank	11.5	NA	15.0
MN	Minneapolis	First National Bank	12.0	NA	12.0
MO	Kansas City	Boatmans First National	13.5	13.3	NA
		Commerce Bank	10.7	NA	12.5

Table 2 continued
*CONSUMER LOAN RATES (AUGUST 1985)**

State	*City*	*Bank*	*48-Mo. New Car*	*120-Mo. Mobile Home*	*24-Mo. Personal*
	St. Louis	Centerre Bank	12.5	NA	18.0
		Mercantile Trust Co.	11.0	NA	14.5
MT	Billings	First Interstate Bank	14.0	NA	16.0
NE	Omaha	Norwest Bank	13.5	NA	16.5
NH	Nashua	Indian Head National	13.0	15.0	17.0
NJ	Hackensack	United Jersey Bank	12.0	NA	16.0
	Jersey City	First Jersey National	12.8	NA	16.0
	Plainsfield	United National Bank	12.5	NA	15.0
	Trenton	New Jersey National	12.3	NA	14.5
NY	Albany	Key Bank	12.9	NA	14.5
	Buffalo	Liberty Norstar Bank	13.0	NA	14.5
		Manufacturers & Traders Trust Co.	14.3	15.0	16.3
		Marine Midland Bank	12.7	14.9	14.9
	New York	Bank of New York	12.5	NA	17.5
		Chase Manhattan	15.3	NA	17.0
		Chemical Bank	13.8	NA	16.0
		Irving Trust Co.	14.0	NA	15.3
		Manufacturers Hanover	15.0	NA	15.5

State	City	Bank	48-Mo. New Car	120-Mo. Mobile Home	24-Mo. Personal
		National Westminster	14.5	NA	15.5
	Rochester	Chase Lincoln First Bank	12.0	NA	15.5
		Security Norstar Bank	13.0	15.5	14.5
NC	Charlotte	First Union National	11.8	14.0	15.3
	Lumberton	Southern National Bank of North Carolina	12.5	NA	15.0
	Rocky Mount	Planters National Bank & Trust Co.	11.5	NA	15.0
OH	Akron	Bank One, Akron	13.0	15.0	16.0
		First National Bank	12.5	15.0	18.0
	Cincinnati	Central Trust Co.	12.5	15.0	17.5
		Fifth Third Bank	13.0	17.0	18.0
		First National Bank	11.5	NA	16.0
	Cleveland	Ameritrust Co.	11.9	NA	13.9
		National City Bank	11.6	11.7	15.3
	Columbus	BancOhio National	12.8	NA	15.0
		Bank One, Columbus	12.5	14.0	14.0
		Huntington National	12.5	17.5	14.3
	Dayton	Bank One, Dayton	12.8	NA	19.0

Table 2 continued
*CONSUMER LOAN RATES (AUGUST 1985)**

State	*City*	*Bank*	*48-Mo. New Car*	*120-Mo. Mobile Home*	*24-Mo. Personal*
	Elyria	Lorain County Bank	12.3	14.5	17.3
	Mansfield	Bank One, Mansfield	12.0	14.0	16.0
	Marion	National City Bank	11.3	NA	14.8
	Youngstown	Mahoning National Bank	11.4	16.9	18.0
OK	Oklahoma City	Bank/Oklahoma/ OK City	13.8	NA	18.0
		First National Bank & Trust	13.5	16.0	14.5
		Liberty National Bank & Trust Co.	12.0	NA	15.0
	Tulsa	First National Bank & Trust	12.0	NA	11.8
OR	Portland	First Interstate Bank of Oregon	13.3	NA	16.5
		United States National	13.5	13.8	14.9
PA	Ardmore	Philadelphia National	12.0	NA	15.5
	Bala-Cynwyd	First Pennsylvania	12.3	NA	13.3
	E. Whiteland	Fidelity Bank	11.9	NA	13.0
	Greensburgh	Mellon Bank	12.3	14.8	13.0
	Nuremberg	Hazelton National	12.5	NA	14.0
	Pittsburgh	Pittsburgh National	10.6	NA	11.9

State	City	Bank	48-Mo. New Car	120-Mo. Mobile Home	24-Mo. Personal
		Union National Bank	12.3	15.5	14.0
	Washington	First National Bank & Trust Co.	12.0	15.5	14.5
	Williamsport	Commonwealth Bank & Trust Co.	12.9	14.0	13.0
RI	Providence	Fleet National Bank	13.3	NA	21.0
		Rhode Island Hosp. Trust National Bank	13.3	14.8	17.5
SC	Charleston	Citizens & Southern National Bank	11.4	13.0	18.0
SD	Sioux Falls	First National Bank	13.0	16.0	14.5
TN	Memphis	First Tenn. Bank	13.6	NA	18.6
		Union Planters National	12.3	NA	14.3
	Nashville	First American National	13.2	NA	13.5
		Third National Bank	14.0	NA	15.0
TX	Beaumont	First City National	15.3	NA	17.5
	Corpus Christi	MBank	13.0	NA	12.0
	Dallas	Interfirst Bank	13.0	NA	17.0
		MBank	13.0	NA	15.6
	Fort Worth	Interfirst Bank	13.5	16.5	18.0
		Texas American Bank	12.8	17.3	16.8
	Harlingen	Interfirst Bank	13.5	15.5	16.5

Table 2 continued
*CONSUMER LOAN RATES (AUGUST 1985)**

State	*City*	*Bank*	*48-Mo. New Car*	*120-Mo. Mobile Home*	*24-Mo. Personal*
	Houston	First City National	13.0	NA	15.0
	San Antonio	National Bank of Fort Sam Houston	11.9	NA	15.5
	Victoria	First Victoria National	14.3	NA	13.5
UT	Salt Lake City	Continental Bank & Trust	13.5	15.0	17.0
VA	Henrico County	Dominion Bank, Richmond	12.5	NA	15.5
	Richmond	Central Fidelity Bank	11.8	NA	17.0
		Sovran Bank	11.8	15.0	17.0
		United Virginia Bank	11.9	NA	16.0
	Roanoke County	Colonial-American National	12.5	NA	14.0
		Dominion Bank	13.3	NA	16.1
	Vienna	Dominion Bank of Northern Virginia	11.5	NA	14.0
WA	Seattle	Peoples National Bank of Washington	12.8	15.5	15.5
		Ranier National Bank	14.3	NA	NA
		Seattle-First National	12.2	14.9	17.0
	Spokane	First Interstate Bank of Washington	13.3	15.0	14.8
WV	Charleston	Charleston National	13.3	NA	17.0

State	City	Bank	48-Mo. New Car	120-Mo. Mobile Home	24-Mo. Personal
		National Bank of Commerce	12.5	NA	18.0
	Huntington	First Huntington National	12.0	NA	14.0
	Princeton	First Community Bank	12.5	11.8	15.0
WI	Milwaukee	First Wisconsin National	12.3	NA	15.5
		Marshall & Isley Bank	12.5	15.0	15.0
	Sheboygan	Security First National	12.4	NA	NA
WY	Casper	Norwest Bank	13.5	NA	15.5

* Cities in the names of banks are usually not included when the bank is in that city.

Variable-Rate Loans

An increasing number of lending institutions offer variable-rate loans. The rates of these loans vary depending on changes in the index used by the institution. At most institutions, the index is based on fluctuations in some external interest rate, such as three-month Treasury notes. But at some banks and S & Ls it is tied to the institution's own cost of funds. Variable-rate loans at these institutions should always be avoided, because, even if most interest rates are declining, the institution can increase its own cost of funds by, for example, raising rates paid on money market funds and certificates of deposit.

Until recently, variable rates were always lower than fixed rates. This was because institutions assumed there was a greater chance of rates rising substantially than falling significantly. A 1984 survey revealed most variable-rate forty-eight-month new-car loans to be one to two percentage points less than comparable fixed-rate loans at specific institutions.

More recently, however, some institutions concluded that rates were more likely to fall than rise and, consequently, began charging higher variable than fixed rates on consumer loans. In August 1985, for example, San Francisco Consumer Action found that First National Bank was charging one percentage point more, and Union Bank one-half a percentage point more on four-year $10,000 variable-rate car loans than on fixed-rate loans.

Because there is far less chance that rates will skyrocket in three or four years than in fifteen to thirty, variable-rate consumer loans are much less risky than variable-rate mortgage loans. If you are prepared to assume some risk, you may well pay significantly lower interest charges on variable-rate loans priced below those with fixed rates. If you are on a tight budget, however, variable-rate loans may make financial planning more difficult.

Other Charges

■ Credit Life and Accident and Health Insurance.

Lenders cannot legally require you to purchase credit life and accident and health insurance with a loan, but some may pressure you to do so. Credit life insurance pays off the loan if you die, thus protecting your family. Accident and health covers payments when your principal income is cut off because of illness or disability.

When you purchase this insurance, charges are usually added to your loan principal. These can be substantial, considerably escalating the cost of your loan. In a survey of credit life and accident and health insurance premiums on a four-year $8000 new-car loan, we found considerable variation in charges. Credit life insurance premiums ranged from a low of $96 to a high of $348. Accident and health charges ranged from a low of $28 to a high of $437.

There are two problems with these two types of insurance. One is that the pay-out ratio tends to be lower than for other types of insurance, not infrequently below 50%. This means that less than half of all premiums collected are returned to policyholders as claims paid.

The second problem is that many families do not need the protection this insurance provides. In the event of death or disability, they can use some other source to pay off the loan—life insurance or disability insurance, a savings account or other liquid assets. You should only consider purchasing this costly insurance if you are without other insurance coverage or adequate savings.

■ Service Charges.

On car loans, many banks charge a nominal amount for acquiring a security interest in the automobile. Typically, this amount is less than $10. Yet a small number of lenders have begun assessing much larger "processing" or "application" fees. These were first identified by Consumer Action surveys of Bay Area financial institutions. This consumer group uncovered fees ranging from $20 to $100, which were not always included in the annual percentage rate that was quoted.

■ Late-Payment Fees.

Banks and finance companies usually assess penalties for making late payments. They add on late charges when they receive a payment more than ten days after its due date. These charges vary considerably among institutions. Typical late fees are $5, $10, 5%, $5 or 5% whichever is less, and $5 or 5% whichever is greater. Clearly, the least expensive charge is $5 or 5% whichever is less. The charge for a delinquent $200 monthly payment is only $5. One bank we surveyed assessed a fee of 10%. At this institution, the late charge on a $200 payment would be $20. At this rate, the charges for several delinquent payments would be considerable.

■ Prepayment Penalties.

Most banks penalize borrowers for early payment of installments. If the loan is paid off shortly after it is contracted, many will charge a penalty that may range from $10 to $50. If it is paid off after a number of payments have been made, many will not assess this penalty but will not completely eliminate outstanding finance charges. This is sanctioned by the Rule of 78, a method of computing the rebate on finance charges. On the other hand, institutions using the actuarial method will rebate all these charges. Recently, several states banned the use of the Rule of 78 in consumer credit. Federal credit unions are also prohibited from using this method.

How to Borrow

After deciding what kind of institution to borrow from, shop around for the cheapest loan. This can be done by calling several lenders to ask about rates. Make sure you tell the lender the size of the loan, the size of the down payment, the length of the loan, and its purpose. The best indicator of price is not the monthly payment, but the annual percentage rate (APR), which takes into consideration all interest and most other charges. The Truth-in-Lending Act requires lenders to disclose the APR in writing.

Do not be afraid to "haggle." Many lenders will charge you less than the quoted rate if you negotiate with them. Do not hesitate to mention that another lender you have talked to offers lower rates.

Also keep in mind that banks may provide discounts to borrowers with checking accounts at their institution and to those who preauthorize monthly payments. In California, each of these discounts is typically worth one-quarter of 1%.

Read the loan agreement before signing. If you are not certain you understand what it says, have an experienced lawyer look at it to make certain it says what you were told verbally. Remember that in court, what counts is what is on paper, not what was said.

Nonpayment: Creditor Remedies and Debtor Options

Banks and other lenders may do more than assess late charges when you miss loan payments. Thirty days after failure to make payment, or sometimes sooner, depending on the type of loan, lenders may accelerate your debt, making the entire sum immediately "due and payable," then take steps to collect this obligation. Even before going to court, they may employ two collection procedures.

■ Acceleration and Offset.

Lenders may attach an account you have maintained at that bank. This "right of offset" allows a bank to recover an unpaid installment loan by collecting the money from your savings or checking account. Since one bank cannot attach the accounts in another bank without going to court, if you are not borrowing specifically on a savings account or CD, you should consider borrowing from a different institution from the one where you maintain checking and savings accounts.

■ Repossession.

Lenders may recover the collateral or security for your loan. On car loans, this "right of repossession" allows the creditor to seize your automobile, sell it in a private sale, deduct the auction price from the debt, add costs of repossession and any necessary repairs, then require you to pay the remaining "deficiency balance."

For instance, if you owe $3000 on a used-car loan and miss payments, your creditor may take your car, sell it for $2000, deduct the $2000 from the $3000 debt, add $70 for repossession costs, add $130 for repairs, then sue to collect the remaining $1200 balance. If you had put $500 down and made $1000 of payments over a one-year period (the time you drove the car), you will have paid $2700 (the down payment plus payments and deficiency balance) for the use of a used car for only one year. Although this illustration is hypothetical, it is not atypical.

■ Judgments and Wage Garnishment.

If you do not pay a deficiency balance, your creditor may sue to collect it. If you believe your debt is not owed or not justified, you should seek assistance. If you have not received notification of a lawsuit, you can enlist the support of either a consumer agency or an attorney. If you have received such notification, you should visit an attorney.

■ Debtor Options.

If you recognize the legitimacy of your debt, you should attempt to prevent litigation by working out a payment schedule that is acceptable to your creditor. You can either try to work out such an agreement on your own or request the assistance of a consumer agency to negotiate with your creditor.

If you cannot meet the payment schedules acceptable to your creditor, you should consider seeking the assistance of a local consumer-credit counseling service. This agency will work out a payment plan that will limit payments to a percentage of your income. You must allow the service to receive your pay checks and make these payments. Although not required to do so, most creditors accept the plan.

A last resort, if you have crushing debts, is bankruptcy. You should resort to this only if you have huge debts, no hope of repaying them, and the assistance of a competent attorney.

CHECKLIST

Use this checklist to compare lending institutions.

Amount borrowed __________

Number of payments __________

Monthly payment __________

Annual percentage rate (APR) __________

Is this rate variable? __________

  If so, how is it indexed? __________

Service fees not included in APR __________

Late-payment fee __________

  When charged? __________

Method of prepayment

  Rule of 78 __________

  Simple interest __________

  Other __________

$ ¢ $ ¢ $

¢ $ ¢ $ ¢

$ ¢ $ ¢ $

¢ $ ¢ $ ¢

9

Credit Cards and Other Charge Cards

RECOMMENDATIONS

Use credit cards and other charge cards to make purchases conveniently, but not to finance them. Because of high interest rates, you should pay balances before finance charges are assessed.

If you regularly pay balances promptly and in full, look for cards that provide a float period, assess no transaction charges, and assess a relatively low annual fee. If you are not able to pay in full promptly, look for a card with these features and with a low interest rate. Secured credit cards offered by S & Ls usually charge rates significantly below those assessed by banks. Even unsecured cards sold by S & Ls often carry somewhat lower rates.

Premium cards, such as MasterCard Gold, Visa Premium, American Express Gold Card, and American Express Platinum

continued on next page

continued

Card, cost more than standard cards, but offer no significant additional benefits to *most* consumers. As a rule, we do not recommend them.

Retain the smallest number of credit and charge cards you need to make desired purchases. This will reduce service charges, the number of monthly bills to be paid, and the inconvenience of reporting any cards that are lost or stolen. Most consumers, for example, have no need for both a MasterCard and a Visa. Similarly, most with an American Express card do not need any other travel and entertainment card.

Credit and charge cards are used most frequently to purchase goods and services. They are safer to carry than cash, provide more leverage in payment disputes than cash, are easier to carry than checks, and out of town are more readily accepted than checks. Cards also serve as useful identification in cashing checks. Some cards can be used to obtain cash.

The principal risk of credit cards is that if balances are not promptly paid in full (and sometimes even if they are), relatively large finance charges are assessed. Along with annual fees and any special fees, these interest charges raise the cost of financing purchases with credit cards significantly above that of installment loans. In 1983, the fees and charges on all charge cards cost consumers an average of more than $200 per family.

Types of Cards

There are three major types of charge cards: bank cards, retailer charge cards, and travel and entertainment cards. They differ by the type of institution that offers them, their acceptance by retailers, and their ability to be used to finance purchases.

■ Bank Cards.

Bank cards are offered by banks, S & Ls, and some credit unions. They represent a widely accepted means of payment, not just in the United States, but also in other countries. These cards allow holders to carry over a balance from month to month. After any grace period (also called "float"), interest charges are assessed.

The two major bank cards are MasterCard and Visa. Most banks and many S & Ls offer one or the other, sometimes both. It is important to remember that many institutions set their own credit terms—credit limit, billing policy, annual fee, and interest rates. In fact, the terms of a MasterCard offered by one bank may be more similar to those of a Visa sold by another than to a MasterCard offered by a third institution. Yet a number of institutions sell the cards of some other institution. In California, for example, several institutions market Marine Midland cards under their own name.

Many California S & Ls offer a unique type of MasterCard or Visa—one secured by a deposit such as a passbook savings account or a certificate of deposit. Cardholders can make purchases only on that portion of deposited funds used as security, often half of the total deposit. However, rates charged on unpaid balances with this type of card are lower than those charged on unsecured bank cards.

Some credit unions also offer credit cards. Usually, these cards do not have an annual fee and carry lower rates than bank cards. However, they often have no float period.

■ Retailer Charge Cards.

These charge cards differ from bank cards primarily in their acceptance. Their use is limited to the issuing retailer or, in the case of some oil company cards, only to select gasoline service stations. A J. C. Penney's card, for example, can be used only at Penney's. Yet, like bank cards, balances can be carried from month to month. Most retailer credit cards are available from department stores or from major oil companies, and have no annual fee.

Recently Sears introduced a credit card called "Discover" that is intended to compete with bank cards. Although its acceptance by retailers is growing rapidly, at present this card can be used only at a small fraction of the establishments that accept MasterCard and Visa. It does, however, permit withdrawals and savings deposits through the ATMs of banks with whom Sears has made a special arrangement.

■ Travel and Entertainment (T & E) Cards.

Like bank cards, travel and entertainment cards are widely accepted in the United States and in other countries. But unlike bank cards, they do not permit holders to carry over balances. Failing to pay balances promptly can lead to cancelation of the card.

The three major T & E cards are American Express, Diners Club, and Carte Blanche. American Express is accepted by nearly twice as many establishments as each of the other two.

■ Standard vs. Premium Cards.

The three major charge cards—MasterCard, Visa, and American Express—offer two or three different types of cards. The most popular is the standard type—MasterCard, Visa Classic, and American Express Personal (the green card). Also available are MasterCard Gold, Visa Premium, American Express Gold Card, and American Express Platinum Card. These premium cards offer a higher credit limit and sometimes ancillary features, such as higher travel-accident insurance and special hotel services. But they also cost more. Typically, their annual fee is about twice that of the standard card. The fee for the Platinum Card is even higher—currently $250.

Unless the premium cards offer special services you especially desire, avoid them. In almost all cases, the credit limit of the standard cards will meet your financial needs. Most MasterCard and Visa card holders, for example, need only the $1000 to $2500 limit provided by standard cards by most banks. Moreover, you may be wise to avoid the temptation of a large credit line.

Charges

■ Interest.

Most credit card related charges represent interest payments—more than $12 billion in 1983. The Truth-in-Lending Act requires credit card issuers to disclose not only the annual percentage rate (APR) of this interest, but also the method of calculating it and the point when the finance charges are first assessed—from the date of sale, posting, billing, or specified period after billing, usually thirty days.

Most banks and retailers still charge a fixed rate. Yet an increasing number charge a variable rate that is indexed to some other rate. A bank card rate, for example, might be set at six percentage points above the six-month Treasury note rate. Since these variable rates approximate fixed rates, and since cards can be canceled at any time, variable rates on credit cards do not subject cardholders to significant risk.

In some states, bank card rates decline in stages as the unpaid balance increases. This rate variation usually reflects state usury laws, which permit higher rates to be charged on smaller balances. Still, holders of bank cards and retailer charge cards in most states pay only one rate at a given institution.

These rates escalated shortly after increases in interest rates in the late 1970s and early 1980s. Even though interest rates in general have declined substantially in the past three years, credit card rates have been lowered by only a few institutions. Our survey and one conducted by *Consumer Reports* yielded the same results—a range from 12% to 22%, with most rates clustered between 18% and 20%. A more recent Federal Reserve survey of member banks reported a range of from 14.5% to 22%. Rates at specific institutions are given on the following pages.

If large balances are carried forward unpaid, the difference in interest charges among institutions can be significant. On a $1000

Table 1
*CREDIT CARD LOAN RATES (AUGUST 1985)**

State	*City*	*Bank*	*Rate (%)*
AL	Birmingham	AmSouth Bank	19.5
AK	Anchorage	National Bank of Alaska	18.0
AZ	Phoenix	First Interstate Bank of Arizona	21.0
AR	Little Rock	Worthen Bank & Trust Co.	NA
CA	Los Angeles	First Interstate Bank of California	21.0
		Union Bank	19.8
	San Francisco	Bank of America	19.8
		Bank of California	21.0
		Crocker National Bank	21.0
		Wells Fargo Bank	20.0
CO	Denver	First Interstate Bank	18.0
		United Bank	21.0
CT	Hartford	Conn. Bank and Trust Co.	18.0
	New Britain	New Britain National Bank	18.0
DC	Washington	Riggs National Bank	NA
		Security National Bank	NA
FL	Fort Myers	First National Bank	NA
	Hialeah	Consolidated Bank	18.0
	Miami	Southeast Bank	18.0
	Orlando	Barnett Bank of Central Florida	18.0
	Stuart	First National Bank & Trust Co.	18.0
	Tampa	First National Bank of Florida	18.0
GA	Atlanta	First National Bank	NA
		National Bank of Georgia	18.0
		Trust Co. Bank	18.0
	Augusta	Georgia Railroad Bank & Trust Co.	18.0
	Macon	Trust Co. Bank of Middle Georgia	18.0
	Savannah	Citizens & Southern National Bank	18.0
IL	Aurora	Aurora National Bank	18.0
	Chicago	Continental Illinois	NA

State	City	Bank	Rate (%)
		First National Bank	19.8
		Harris Trust & Savings	19.8
		La Salle National Bank	NA
		Merchandise National	18.0
		Northern Trust Co.	NA
	Peoria	First National Bank	NA
IN	Evansville	Citizens National Bank	21.0
	Fort Wayne	Lincoln National Bank & Trust Co.	18.0
	Indianapolis	American Fletcher National Bank	19.8
		Indiana National Bank	19.8
		Merchants National Bank & Trust Co.	19.8
IA	Des Moines	Norwest Bank	19.8
	Sioux City	Security National Bank	NA
KS	Topeka	First National Bank	NA
KY	Louisville	Citizens Fidelity Bank & Trust Co.	18.0
		First National Bank	18.0
LA	Lafayette	First National Bank	18.0
MD	Baltimore	First National Bank of Maryland	NA
		Maryland National Bank	NA
		Union Trust Co. of Md.	18.8
MA	Andover	Baybank Merrimack Valley	18.0
	Boston	Bank of New England	16.8
		First National Bank	17.0
		Shawmut Bank	17.0
		State Street Bank & Trust Co.	18.0
	Worcester	Shawmut Worcester City Bank	17.0
MI	Detroit	Comerica Bank	18.0
		First of American Bank	18.0
		Manufacturers National	18.0
		National Bank	18.0
	Grand Rapids	Old Kent Bank and Trust Co.	18.0
	Lansing	Michigan National Bank	18.0
	Marquette	First National Bank & Trust Co.	18.0

Table 1 continued
*CREDIT CARD LOAN RATES (AUGUST 1985)**

State	*City*	*Bank*	*Rate (%)*
	Mount Clemens	First National Bank in Mt. Clemens	18.0
	Pontiac	Community National Bank	18.0
MN	Minneapolis	First National Bank	19.8
MO	Kansas City	Boatmans First National	NA
		Commerce Bank	22.0
	St. Louis	Centerre Bank	22.0
		Mercantile Trust Co.	19.8
MT.	Billings	First Interstate Bank	NA
NE	Omaha	Norwest Bank	NA
NH	Nashua	Indian Head National	18.0
NJ	Hackensack	United Jersey Bank	18.0
	Jersey City	First Jersey National	18.0
	Plainfield	United National Bank	18.0
	Trenton	New Jersey National	19.0
NY	Albany	Key Bank	18.0
	Buffalo	Liberty Norstar Bank	18.0
		Manufacturers & Traders Trust Co.	19.8
		Marine Midland Bank	19.8
	New York	Bank of New York	NA
		Chase Manhattan	19.8
		Chemical Bank	19.5
		Irving Trust Co.	19.8
		Manufacturers Hanover	19.8
		National Westminster	19.8
	Rochester	Chase Lincoln First Bank	19.5
		Security Norstar Bank	18.0
NC	Charlotte	First Union National	18.0
	Lumberton	Southern National Bank of North Carolina	18.0

State	City	Bank	Rate (%)
	Rocky Mount	Planters National Bank & Trust Co.	18.0
OH	Akron	Bank One, Akron	21.6
		First National Bank	18.0
	Cincinnati	Central Trust Co.	21.0
		Fifth Third Bank	19.8
		First National Bank	19.8
	Cleveland	Ameritrust Co.	18.0
		National City Bank	15.6
	Columbus	BancOhio National	19.8
		Bank One Columbus	21.6
		Huntington National	21.6
	Dayton	Bank One, Dayton	18.0
	Elyria	Lorain County Bank	18.0
	Mansfield	Bank One, Mansfield	21.6
	Marion	National City Bank	15.6
	Youngstown	Mahoning National Bank	18.0
OK	Oklahoma City	Bank/Oklahoma/OK City	18.0
		First National Bank & Trust	14.5
		Liberty National Bank & Trust Co.	18.0
	Tulsa	First National Bank & Trust	NA
OR	Portland	First Interstate Bank of Oregon	21.0
		United States National	19.3
PA	Ardmore	Philadelphia National	NA
	Bala-Cynwyd	First Pennsylvania	NA
	E. Whiteland	Fidelity Bank	18.0
	Greensburgh	Mellon Bank	18.6
	Nuremberg	Hazelton National	18.0
	Pittsburgh	Pittsburgh National	NA
		Union National Bank	18.0
	Washington	First National Bank & Trust Co.	18.0
	Williamsport	Commonwealth Bank & Trust Co.	NA

Table 1 continued
*CREDIT CARD LOAN RATES (AUGUST 1985)**

State	*City*	*Bank*	*Rate (%)*
RI	Providence	Fleet National Bank	21.0
		Rhode Island Hosp. Trust National Bank	17.8
SC	Charleston	Citizens & Southern National Bank	21.0
SD	Sioux Falls	First National Bank	16.0
TN	Memphis	First Tenn. Bank	21.0
		Union Planters National	21.0
	Nashville	First American National	20.0
		Third National Bank	20.0
TX	Beaumont	First City National	NA
	Corpus Christi	MBank	18.0
	Dallas	Interfirst Bank	16.5
		MBank	NA
	Fort Worth	Interfirst Bank	NA
		Texas American Bank	16.5
	Harlingen	Interfirst Bank	16.5
	Houston	First City National	NA
	San Antonio	National Bank of Fort Sam Houston	15.0
	Victoria	First Victoria National	18.0
UT	Salt Lake City	Continental Bank & Trust	18.0
VA	Henrico County	Dominion Bank, Richmond	18.0
	Richmond	Central Fidelity Bank	18.0
		Sovran Bank	18.0
		United Virginia Bank	18.0
	Roanoke County	Colonial-American National	18.0
		Dominion Bank	18.0
	Vienna	Dominion Bank of Northern Virginia	18.0
WA	Seattle	Peoples National Bank of Washington	15.5

State	City	Bank	Rate (%)
		Ranier National Bank	15.0
		Seattle-First National	15.0
	Spokane	First Interstate Bank of Washington	18.0
WV	Charleston	Charleston National	18.0
		National Bank of Commerce	18.0
	Huntington	First Huntington National	18.0
	Princeton	First Community Bank	NA
WI	Milwaukee	First Wisconsin National	18.0
		Marshall & Illsley Bank	18.0
	Sheboygan	Security First National	NA
WY	Casper	Norwest Bank	NA

* Cities in the names of banks are usually not included when the bank is in that city.

average balance, a 22% rate imposes annual charges of $220, but a 15% rate only $150.

The size of these charges reflects not only the rate, but also the way in which it is computed. Two factors are important here: one is when the interest begins to be charged to your account; the other is how finance charges are calculated.

Most credit card issuers continue to provide thirty grace days (also called a "float" period). Yet, increasingly, institutions have begun restricting this period, and in a few instances have eliminated it entirely. Avoid using cards from banks and retailers that have done so.

The major difference between the three most popular methods of calculating finance charges is whether you get immediate credit for payments made during the billing period. Under the adjusted-method balance you do. Under the previous-balance method you do not. And under the average daily-balance method you might. The third method has become the most popular. Keep in mind that the method of calculating interest will not affect you if bills are paid in full during the grace period.

■ Annual Fee.

For cardholders who pay balances in full, the most significant charge is the annual fee. For standard national cards, our survey revealed a range from zero (Twin City Federal, Minneapolis) to $50 (Fidelity Federal, Los Angeles). Most banks charge between $15 and $20 for MasterCards and Visa cards. Currently, American Express charges $45. Financial institutions in Texas and Missouri are not permitted to assess annual fees, but tend to charge higher interest rates and may restrict or eliminate grace days.

Periodically, Bank Card Holders of America issues a list of banks without annual fees. Table 2 lists institutions that offered major cards without an annual fee in June 1985. All these banks (only institutions that members of Bank Card Holders have called to the attention of the organization) provide cards with grace periods that are not restricted to depositors. For a more current list, contact Bank Card Holders of America by calling 1-800-638-6407 or by writing to the organization at 333 Pennsylvania Avenue, S.E., Washington, D.C. 20003.

Table 2
BANKS WITH NO ANNUAL CREDIT CARD FEE (JUNE 1985)

Bank	*Location*	*Card*	*Eligibility*
Avco National	Irvine, CA	MC, V	No restrictions
Bank of Baltimore	Baltimore, MD	MC, V	All MD and DC; parts of PA, DE, VA
CCNB	New Cumberland, PA	MC, V	South-central PA
Fidelity National	Atlanta, GA	MC, V	GA
Imperial Savings	San Diego, CA	V	No restrictions
The More Card	Evansville, IN	V	No restrictions
Standard Federal Bank	Troy, MI	V	MI and IN
Valley National	Bogota, NJ	MC, V	Northern NJ

■ Transaction Charges.

The large majority of charge card issuers do not assess fees for charge card purchases. Yet a small and apparently growing number have begun to do so. Crocker National in San Francisco, for example, charges $.12 per transaction.

If this minimum payment is not made in a specified period of time, a fee is assessed. In our survey, this charge was typically 5% or $10. For those with large balances, the percentage charge could be substantial—$50 on a $1000 balance. The period of time card holders were given to make the minimum payment before the fee was assessed ranged from ten to twenty days.

■ Fee for Exceeding Credit Limit.

Some institutions in our survey imposed no special charges for exceeding the credit limit. They simply charged interest on the entire balance and decided whether to cancel the card. Other banks assessed a penalty that ranged from $5 to $15.

■ Charge for Paying Bills in Full.

About one-third of all credit card users pay off their balance in full each month, thus avoiding interest charges. A few banks penalize those who pay off their balances promptly, by levying a fee. At Centerre Bank in St. Louis, this charge goes up to $4 a month; at People's National in Seattle, it is $1; at First National in Omaha, it is 2% or $1.75, whichever is less. We recommend you avoid cards with these charges.

■ Charge for Cash Advance.

Most banks charge interest on cash advances at the same rate as credit purchases, but cash advance charges begin from the date of the advance. Many institutions now assess an additional charge that is either a fixed amount, typically, $2 to $3, or a percentage of the amount borrowed, usually 2% to 5%. On large cash advances, of course, the percentage fee can be much larger than the set amount. Also, if the cash advance is not paid in full in the next billing period, it may trigger interest charges on subsequent credit purchases.

How to Read Your Monthly Bill

Monthly bills for various cards look different, but contain the same kinds of information.

First look for the amount owed and the payment due date. Do not confuse the amount owed with the minimum payment due.

Second, check the list of purchases made with the card and any cash advances. Do not be afraid to question a purchase you do not think you made. On most bills there is a telephone number you can call and address you can write to.

Third, look for finance charges and other charges. Finance charges are usually listed in a row of figures that includes previous balance, new purchases, cash advances, payments, and new balance. Other fees are usually listed along with specific transactions. Again, if you question any of these charges, do not hesitate to call or write the card company.

Other information you should note includes the total credit limit and what is currently available, the statement period, the interest rate, the method of computing interest charges, and, on some statements, your billing rights.

The following pages show a copy of a Visa bill with arrows indicating where much of this information is found.

Related Services

Credit card companies are increasingly offering services beyond credit purchases and cash advances to cardholders. American Express has pioneered in this area, but banks like Citicorp have also begun to offer a variety of ancillary services. These are described below.

■ Cash.

American Express guarantees personal checks at its offices and at many banks, hotels, motels, and airline counters. The maximum amount of the check depends on the type of card held and the place where the check is cashed. Premium cardholders can cash larger checks than can green card holders. The largest checks can be cashed at the more than 1000 American Express Travel offices world-wide.

An increasing number of banks are making cash available to credit cardholders through their own automated teller machines (ATMs) and those of other institutions. Citicorp's Choice cardholders, for example, now can withdraw cash from 240 teller machines in the Denver area. Within several years, holders of most major credit cards will be able to get cash in most major metropolitan areas and in some other areas as well.

■ Discounts.

Charge card companies are increasingly offering goods and services at a discount. Some banks have begun to sell items such as televisions and telephones at discounted prices to credit card customers. American Express makes available reduced rates for hotel rooms and car rentals to Gold and Platinum cardholders.

These discounts are, however, often from list prices for brand-name merchandise. Many items are available at even lower prices from some retailers.

■ Travel and Insurance.

American Express Gold and Platinum cardholders receive special travel services not available to other travelers. These include access to a twenty-four-hour toll-free number staffed by personnel who will make or alter travel arrangements on the spot. All American Express cardholders are also provided $100,000 of free travel accident insurance when tickets are charged on their cards. For an

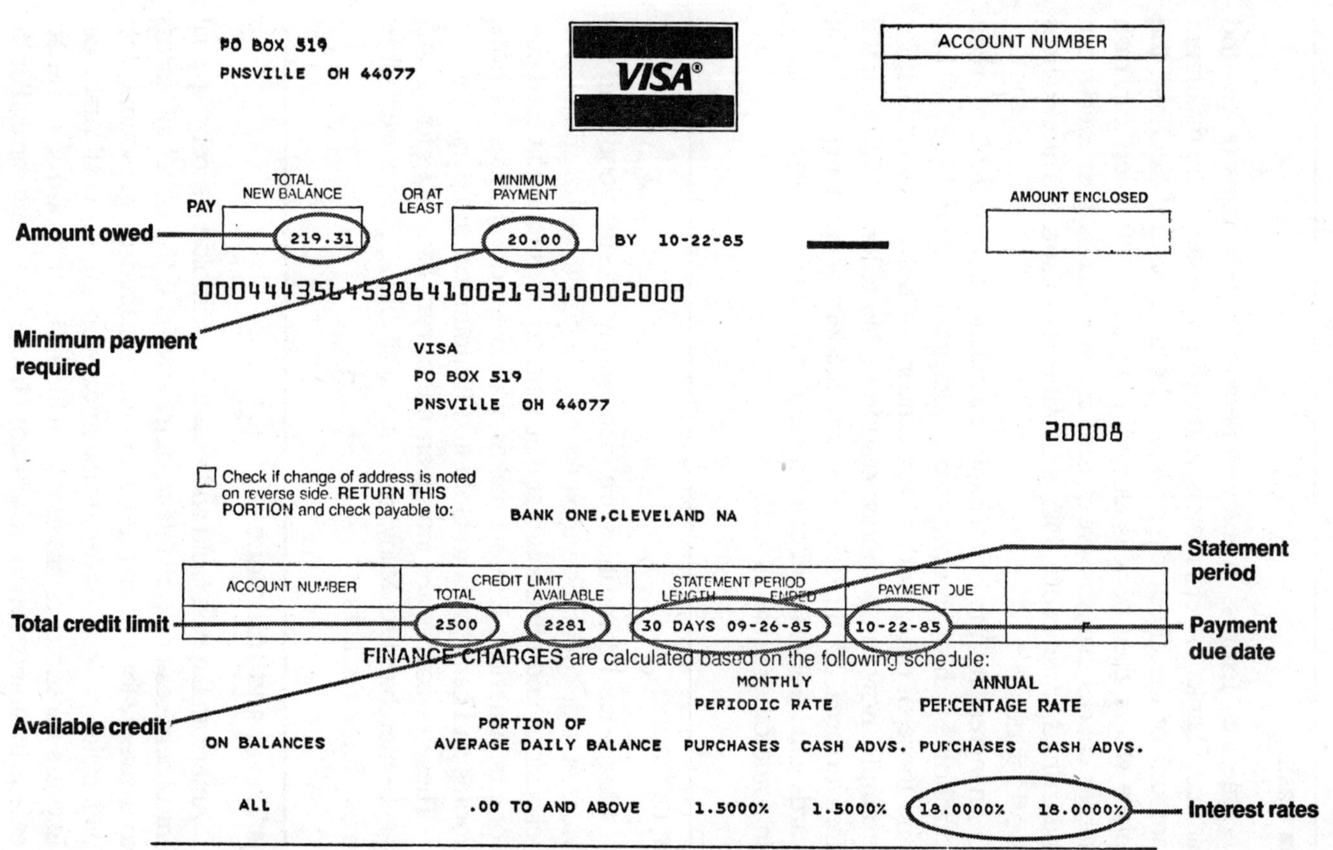
PO BOX 519
PNSVILLE OH 44077

VISA®

ACCOUNT NUMBER

PAY	TOTAL NEW BALANCE	OR AT LEAST	MINIMUM PAYMENT		AMOUNT ENCLOSED
	219.31		20.00	BY 10-22-85	

000444356453864100219310002000

VISA
PO BOX 519
PNSVILLE OH 44077

20008

☐ Check if change of address is noted on reverse side. RETURN THIS PORTION and check payable to: BANK ONE,CLEVELAND NA

ACCOUNT NUMBER	CREDIT LIMIT TOTAL	CREDIT LIMIT AVAILABLE	STATEMENT PERIOD LENGTH	STATEMENT PERIOD ENDED	PAYMENT DUE	
	2500	2281	30 DAYS	09-26-85	10-22-85	

FINANCE CHARGES are calculated based on the following schedule:

ON BALANCES	PORTION OF AVERAGE DAILY BALANCE	MONTHLY PERIODIC RATE PURCHASES	MONTHLY PERIODIC RATE CASH ADVS.	ANNUAL PERCENTAGE RATE PURCHASES	ANNUAL PERCENTAGE RATE CASH ADVS.
ALL	.00 TO AND ABOVE	1.5000%	1.5000%	18.0000%	18.0000%

TO AVOID ADDITIONAL FINANCE CHARGES ON THE NEW BALANCE OF PURCHASES, PAY THE FULL AMOUNT BY THE DATE PAYMENT DUE. IF THE FULL AMOUNT IS NOT PAID, FINANCE CHARGES WILL BE INCURRED FROM THE STATEMENT DATE ON THE AVERAGE DAILY PRINCIPAL BALANCE OF PREVIOUSLY BILLED BUT UNPAID PURCHASES, AND ON NEW PURCHASES FROM THE DATE SUCH NEW PURCHASES ARE POSTED TO YOUR ACCOUNT. FINANCE CHARGES WILL BE INCURRED ON THE AVERAGE DAILY PRINCIPAL BALANCE OF CASH ADVANCES FROM THE DATE POSTED TO YOUR ACCOUNT UNTIL PAYMENT IN FULL IS ENTERED TO YOUR ACCOUNT. AVERAGE DAILY PRINCIPAL BALANCES ARE CALCULATED SEPARATELY BY DIVIDING THE SUM OF THE OUTSTANDING DAILY BALANCES OF PURCHASES AND CASH ADVANCES, MINUS UNPAID FINANCE CHARGES AND FEES, BY THE NUMBER OF DAYS IN THE STATEMENT PERIOD. FINANCE CHARGES WHICH ACCRUE USING THIS CALCULATION WILL APPEAR ON YOUR NEXT STATEMENT.

16

	FINANCE CHARGE	AVERAGE DAILY BALANCE	ANNUAL PERCENTAGE RATE
PURCHASE	.00	.00	18.0000%
CASH ADVANCE	.00	.00	18.0000%

ANNUAL PERCENTAGE RATE FOR STATEMENT PERIOD ENDING 10/05 IS 15.91 % APR

	PREVIOUS BALANCE	NEW PURCHASES AND ADVANCES	PAYMENTS	CREDITS, FEES & ADJS (NET)	FINANCE CHARGE	NEW BALANCE
PURCHASE	660.04	219.31	660.04-	.00	.00	219.31
CASH ADVANCE	.00	.00	.00-	.00	.00	.00
TOTAL	660.04	219.31	660.04-	.00	.00	219.31

SEND INQUIRIES TO: PO BOX 519, PNSVILLE OH 44077 PHONE: 1-216-352-5672

T R A N S A C T I O N D E T A I L

REFERENCE	POST DATE	TRAN DATE	DESCRIPTION	CITY	ST	AMOUNT
41460009032466O109	09-04	08-12	ANDERSON STUDIO	EAST BOOTHBAY	ME	18.90
4168000829SA9Y53Y7	08-30	08-20	FRANCONIA INN	FRANCONIA	NH	109.55
43182008282 4056961	08-30	08-24	BREAD & CHOCOLATE INC	WASHINGTON	DC	15.07
43660009169006 1536	09-17	09-09	POLITICS & PROSE BKSTR	WASHINGTON	DC	16.80
43660009209007 6870	09-23	09-11	THAI ROOM RESTAURANT	WASH	DC	13.73
43680009185106 7260	09-19	09-15	APANA	WASHINGTON	DC	45.26
26240926	09-26	09-26	PAYMENT--THANK YOU			660.04-

15615 PAGE 1 OF 1

6

Address for inquiries

Total finance charges

Number for inquiries

Purchases

additional fee, Gold cardholders are provided nonresident memberships in more than eighty-five city, country, and athletic clubs located out of town. Platinum cardholders receive these memberships free.

How to Shop for a Credit Card

As a general rule, the fewer the number of credit cards you hold the better. You will make fewer impulse purchases, have fewer bills to pay, be assessed fewer fees, and suffer less inconvenience if cards are lost or stolen. To limit the number of cards, identify the types of purchases you wish to make with a card, then seek the fewest cards that will permit you to make these purchases.

The most versatile cards are MasterCard and Visa. Each of them is accepted at about 4 million establishments throughout the world. But the terms of these cards vary from bank to bank, so comparative shopping is essential in selecting one. This shopping should begin with, but go beyond, the credit card application and other printed material. Frequently, this material fails to indicate the most important characteristics of different cards, such as the interest rate and when interest is charged. Use the end of this chapter checklist to assist in making a decision.

You should not restrict your shopping to the area where you live or work. Increasingly, banks are marketing their cards nationwide. Cards offered by banks in other areas may have more favorable terms. Because of billing delays, they may also provide a slightly longer float period. Yet keep in mind that it is often more difficult, and expensive, to resolve disputes on cards from out-of-town banks.

How to Use a Credit Card

Once you have obtained a credit card, it is important to take certain precautions. San Francisco Consumer Action recommends the following:

1. Sign your cards as soon as they arrive.

2. Keep your cards in a safe place and carry them separately from your wallet.

3. Keep, in a secure place, a record of your card numbers and expiration dates, and the phone number and address of each card company.

4. Save all records of purchases. Always destroy or void carbon copies of transactions and the carbon paper that made the copies.

5. Never give your credit card numbers out over the phone unless you are sure of a company's legitimacy.

6. Avoid signing a blank receipt.

7. Notify card companies in advance of a change of address.

8. Never lend your cards to anyone.

9. Notify card companies immediately if cards are lost or stolen.

10. Open billing statements promptly and reconcile your card accounts each month.

Problems and Remedies

■ Unsolicited Cards.

It is illegal for a card issuer to send you a credit card unless you ask or apply for one. However, an issuer is allowed to send you an application or solicit you by phone.

■ Delayed Billing.

The Fair Credit Billing Act requires creditors who offer float periods to mail statements no later than fourteen days before the payment is due. Moreover, in most cases they must credit payments on the day these payments are received.

■ Billing Errors.

If you write to the creditor within sixty days after the bill was mailed and pay the portion of the bill not in dispute, the Fair Credit

Billing Act requires the lender to correct your account within ninety days or send you an explanation.

■ Defective Goods.

When you receive a defective product for which you paid with a credit card, the Fair Credit Billing Act usually allows you to withhold payment on the disputed amount until the dispute is resolved. But you must have made an honest effort to resolve the problem with the merchant.

■ Lost or Stolen Credit Cards.

The Truth-in-Lending Act limits your liability when your credit card is lost or stolen. You are not required to pay any unauthorized charges after this loss is reported to the card issuer. Even if you fail to report the loss, the most you can be charged is $50 on each card.

C H E C K L I S T

Use this checklist when shopping for a credit card.

Interest rate information
- Rate
  - For credit purchases ____________
  - For cash advances ____________
- When charged
  - Date of purchase ____________
  - Date of posting ____________
  - 30 days after billing ____________
  - Other ____________

Method of computation
- Adjusted balance ____________
- Previous balance ____________
- Average daily balance ____________

Fee information
- Annual fee ____________
- Cash advance ____________
- Over credit limit ____________
- Transaction charge ____________
- Late payment ____________
- Paying bill in full ____________

Your credit limit ____________

$ ¢ $ ¢ $

¢ $ ¢ $ ¢

$ ¢ $ ¢ $

¢ $ ¢ $ ¢

10

Home Mortgages: A Changing Marketplace

RECOMMENDATIONS

In general, the best way to finance a home is with a conventional fixed-payment mortgage amortized over the fewest possible years. Home buyers should seek out mortgages with low or no loan origination fees (points). The shorter the time a home is owned, the more costly such points are to the borrower. Since most people sell their homes long before they pay off their mortgages, a loan issued at a higher interest rate, but carrying no points, could well be cheaper than a loan with a marginally lower interest rate and several points.

If you plan to own your home for only a few years, adjustable rate mortgages (ARMs) may be appropriate for you. Again, with this arrangement it is important for you to keep points at a minimum. It is also important that there be limits,

continued on next page

continued

or caps, on rate increases. Seek out an ARM that has low caps on both the yearly adjustment and the maximum adjustment over the life of the mortgage. As a guideline, the Federal Housing Administration has authorized lenders to offer ARMs that limit annual adjustments to 1% and limit the total increase during the entire life of the loan to 5%. Always avoid mortgages with capped payments, but no caps on the interest rate.

If you decide to purchase an ARM, exercise a great deal of caution. ARMs are offered at lower rates than conventional mortgages because they shift most of the risk of interest rate changes from the lender to the borrower. As a result, the default rate on ARMs is 45% higher than it is on conventional mortgages. Ask the lender to work up a worst-case scenario, in which rates go up by the maximum each year until the life of the loan cap is reached, then ask yourself if you can afford the higher payments. Unless you are in unusual circumstances (for example, you are a doctor beginning a practice and expect substantially higher income in the near future), you will find that if you can afford the worst-case payments, you can qualify for a conventional mortgage.

It pays to shop extensively for mortgage loans, since rates vary widely within a metropolitan area. It is not uncommon for rates to vary by more than 1%, sometimes by as much as 2%. On a twenty-year $50,000 conventional mortgage, monthly payments for principal and interest are $603.57 if the interest rate is 13.5%, $640.00 if the rate is 14.5%, and $676.94 if the rate is 15.5%. Not only do you pay much more interest at the higher rates, but the difference in payments can make the difference between qualifying for a fixed-rate mortgage and being forced to take an ARM.

Obtaining a mortgage probably will the most important financial transaction of your lifetime. Mortgages are relatively complex financial structures. But because the financial consequences of obtaining a mortgage can be enormous, you would be wise to familiarize yourself with the various mortgages available.

The long-term, fixed-rate, self-amortizing mortgage has been with us for only fifty years. Prior to the 1930s, mortgages resembled commercial loans; large balloon payments were due after about five years. Consequently, particularly during the Great Depression, foreclosure and eviction were common. While the subsequent introduction and growth of conventional mortgages did not abolish foreclosure and eviction, it made home ownership a realizable goal for most Americans. Unfortunately, high and variable long-term interest rates have priced many families out of home markets and have saddled others with mortgage-payment problems.

In recent years, many new types of mortgage loans have been developed by the financial services industry, but one type, the adjustable rate mortgage (ARM), has emerged as the industry favorite. In 1985, more than 50% of all new mortgages were ARMs.

Factors Common to All Mortgages

■ Loan Application Fee.

This is a nonrefundable fee for processing a mortgage application, and is charged by most lenders. The fee can be as high as $300, and is not returned even if the loan application is denied. Therefore, you should try to determine whether you will qualify for the loan you are seeking prior to making formal application. Lending officers will be happy to tell you their credit standards if you ask them.

Table 1 shows the application fees we found in our survey.

■ Loan Origination Fees.

These fees are designed to give the lending institution immediate earnings on its loans. The popularity of origination fees has increased in recent years because institutions need to rebuild their capital positions. These deteriorated badly when interest rates rose

Table 1
LOAN APPLICATION FEES

Amount	*Percent of Institutions*
$0	31
$100–149	11
$150–199	20
$200–249	22
$250–299	9
$300 and over	9

sharply while banks and S & Ls were holding large portfolios of long-term low-rate loans.

Loan origination fees take two forms. One is a fixed dollar amount, which in some cases is charged instead of an application fee or an appraisal fee, but in others is simply an additional charge. Less than one-fourth of the banks in our survey charged such fees. The other type of origination fee is sometimes called a "loan discount fee," and is charged in the form of points. One point is 1% of the loan amount. All but one lender in our survey charged points.

The impact of points and other front-loaded fees is to raise the effective interest rate on loans and increase the amount of money you need to borrow to finance a home. For example, if you want to buy an $80,000 house and have $30,000 in cash, you need to borrow $50,000 if no points or origination fees are charged, or $51,546.39 if three points are charged.

The impact of points on the effective annual interest rate of a loan depends on the period of time the borrower takes to pay off the loan. If the loan is outstanding for fifteen years, a point adds about ⅛% to the effective interest rate. However, if the loan is outstanding for only five years, a point adds ¼% to the effective rate.

The following example illustrates the impact of points on interest rates and monthly payments. Suppose that you are considering alternative mortgages for securing the $50,000 mentioned above. The first carries an interest rate of 12.124% and one point, while the second is offered at 12% with three points. You would have to borrow $50,505.05 to obtain $50,000 for the first loan, and $51,546.39 for the second loan. Monthly payments for the two loans amortized over twenty years would be $560.51 for the first, and $567.57 for the second.

The impact of points is greater if you pay the loan back early. For example, if each of the above loans is paid back after seven years, which is about average for a home mortgage, the 12.125% loan would have an outstanding balance of $43,913.06, while the 12% loan would have an outstanding balance of $44,737.54.

On the other hand, the impact of points is slightly smaller if the loan is amortized over a greater number of years and held to term. If amortized over twenty years, the effective annual interest rate on the 12.125% one-point loan would be 12.29%, whereas the effective rate for the 12% three-point loan would be 12.49%. If amortized over thirty years, the rate on the former would be 12.26% and on the latter 12.41%.

■ Appraisal and Credit Check Fees.

All lenders require that the property you are about to purchase be appraised, so that their loan will be properly secured. This appraisal is usually done by the lending institution, but independent appraisers are also used. Twenty percent of the institutions we surveyed included the cost of appraisal in their application fees. Fees charged separately ranged from a low of $70, at First Federal of Michigan, to a high of $210, at Society in Cleveland (but note that Society has no application fee).

Lenders also run credit checks on applicants and charge them for it in some cases. The fee for this is generally between $25 and $50. Most lenders include this cost as part of their application fee.

■ Title Insurance.

All lenders will require you to pay for title insurance when you finance your home. This insurance protects the lender, not you, in the event an unanticipated incumbrance is brought against your home. Title insurance is obtained from one of several large title insurance companies, and the cost of the insurance, which is a one-time charge, is billed to you. If you wish to protect yourself as well as the lender, you can purchase this added coverage from the same title company for a small additional fee. But this purchase must be made at the same time the lender's insurance is obtained.

■ Minimum Down Payment to Avoid Private Mortgage Insurance.

In order to protect themselves in the event you default on your mortgage, lenders usually require you to make a substantial down payment on the property you wish to purchase. If you are unable to make a large enough down payment, you will be required to purchase private mortgage insurance (PMI), which protects the lender against default. At the time of our survey the cost of PMI was 1% of the loan amount at closing and ¼% of the outstanding principal per year thereafter. On a $50,000 loan, this would add $500 to closing costs and increase monthly payments by about $10. PMI on adjustable rate mortgages is somewhat more expensive, reflecting their higher default rate.

All but one financial institution in our survey required only 20% down to avoid PMI on conventional mortgages. The exception was National Westminster in New York, which required a 25% down payment. A number of lenders required higher down payments to avoid PMI on adjustable rate mortgages, reflecting the higher risk of default on ARMs. Ten percent of lenders required a 30% down payment on ARMs. Two banks, Security Pacific and Bank of America, both in California, will not make ARM loans if minimum down-payment standards are not met.

■ Prepayment Penalties.

There are two reasons you may wish to pay off a mortgage before it is fully amortized. First, you may sell your home to move to another location. On the average, Americans do this about every eight years. Second, you may have a high-rate conventional mortgage and find it advantageous to refinance when interest rates have fallen. In either case, you could be subject to substantial prepayment penalties.

Only 5% of the lenders in our survey assessed prepayment penalties on ARMs. However, 18% charged a prepayment penalty on conventional mortgages. In all cases, if the loan was outstanding for at least five years, no prepayment penalty was assessed.

■ Late-Payment Penalty.

All lenders assessed a late-payment penalty for overdue mortgage payments; generally ten to fifteen grace days are given. The penalty ranged from 3% to 6% on the past due principal and interest. Several institutions had a $5 maximum on this fee, a very desirable feature if you are negligent about bill paying.

■ Assumability.

If you want to sell your house before your mortgage is fully paid off, the assumability of the mortgage can be a valuable selling point if interest rates have risen. Assumability allows the buyer of your home to take over your mortgage under the same terms and conditions. This feature can be worth thousands of dollars to both seller and buyer.

To demonstrate, with the $50,500 twenty-year mortgage at a fixed 12.125% rate, with monthly payments of $560.51 mentioned earlier, if you decide to sell the home after seven years, there will be an outstanding balance of nearly $44,000 on the loan. Assume that interest rates are now 15% for mortgage loans, and that your prospective buyer needs only $44,000 in a loan to buy your home. If the loan can be assumed, the payments remain $560.51. But if the loan must be refinanced at a 15% rate, monthly payments rise by more than $80, to $642.53. The assumability feature of this mortgage is worth about $5,600. In addition, certain closing costs, such as appraisal fees and discount points, may sometimes be avoided, saving an additional several thousand dollars.

The value of assumability for adjustable rate mortgages cannot be determined exactly, due to rate fluctuations. However, assumability is still a valuable feature if the ARM has rate caps. For example, if an ARM was taken out at 10% with a 5% life-of-the-loan cap, and the rates have increased to 15%, the assumable ARM can be adjusted only downward over the remaining life of the loan. The rate on the loan can never go higher, no matter how high interest rates climb, and may fall to as little as 5% if rates decline.

Only 25% of the institutions surveyed allowed conventional mortgages to be assumed by a third party, and in half of the cases there were proviso clauses that limited assumability according to certain rules of the lender. Thirty-eight percent of lenders allowed ARMs to be assumed, but half of them had a proviso clause.

■ Escrow for Taxes and Insurance.

Escrow, or impound accounts, for taxes and insurance were required by over 85% of the lenders in our survey. Under an escrow arrangement, the lender collects one-twelfth of your yearly property taxes and hazard insurance premiums with each mortgage installment payment. The lender then pays these obligations for you when they become due.

Lenders require escrow accounts to protect their security interest in your home. If your house were to burn down and you had let your hazard insurance lapse, all that would remain as security for your mortgage would be the land on which your house once stood. Similarly, if the city took your house and auctioned it because you failed to pay taxes, the lender would be likely to suffer a loss.

Twenty percent of the mortgage lenders in our survey that required escrow accounts did so only if the loan-to-value ratio was more than a certain maximum, generally 80%. About half of the institutions surveyed paid no interest on escrow accounts. The rest paid between 1% and 5.5% on the accounts, with 2% being the most common. These yields are not very attractive, and most borrowers are better off avoiding mortgages that require escrow accounts. On the other hand, lost earnings are not that large. An escrow account with an average balance of $1000 that pays no interest is equivalent to an extra ⅛% on the interest rate of a $50,000 mortgage during its initial five years.

■ Length of Mortgage.

Lenders will write mortgages for as long as thirty years, and most mortgages are for at least fifteen. The average term of new mortgages is over twenty-seven years. Consumers are, in general, better off with the shortest-term mortgage they can afford, because the savings thus realized are very substantial. For example, the total payments on a $50,000 mortgage at 13% are over $85,000 less if it is taken for a fifteen-year term rather than a thirty-year term. Further, it is often possible to get a shorter-term mortgage for a lower rate than one having a longer term. It is not unusual for the rate on a fifteen-year mortgage to be one-half a percentage point lower than the rate on a thirty-year mortgage. In this case, the savings would be almost $90,000 on the loan in the example.

Table 2
15-YEAR VS. 30-YEAR $50,000 MORTGAGE

Interest Rate (%)	*Monthly Payments 15-Year*	*Monthly Payments 30-Year*	*Dollar Difference per Payment*	*Yearly Income to Qualify (in thousands)*	
				15-Yr.	*30-Yr.*
10	$537.30	438.79	98.51	$31.6	$27.4
10.5	552.70	457.37	95.33	32.3	28.2
11	568.30	476.16	92.14	32.9	29.1
11.5	584.09	495.15	88.94	33.6	29.8
12	600.08	514.31	85.77	34.3	30.6
12.5	616.26	533.63	82.63	35.0	31.4
13	632.62	553.10	79.52	35.7	32.3
13.5	649.16	572.71	76.45	36.4	33.1
14	665.87	592.44	73.43	37.1	34.0
14.5	682.75	612.28	70.47	37.8	34.8
15	699.79	632.22	67.57	38.6	35.7
15.5	717.00	652.26	64.74	39.3	36.5
16	734.35	672.38	61.97	40.0	37.4

The advantage of a longer-term mortgage is that monthly payments are lower. For people of modest means, a lower monthly payment can make the difference between qualifying for a loan or not. Table 2 demonstrates the difference in monthly payments and the income required to qualify for a $50,000 mortgage at different interest rates, assuming that property taxes and hazard insurance premiums on the home total $200 a month, and using 28%, the industry standard for the qualifying ratio of home-ownership payments (the total of mortgage payment, property tax payment, and hazard insurance premiums) to gross monthly income.

As can be seen, differences in monthly payments between fifteen- and thirty-year mortgages are relatively small, and get smaller at higher rates of interest. Further, if the fifteen-year mortgage can be obtained for a rate that is half a percentage point lower than the thirty-year mortgage, the difference is even smaller. Comparing a fifteen-year mortgage at 12.5% and a thirty-year mortgage at 13% reveals a difference of only $63 in monthly payments, and a difference of only $2700 in income to qualify.

Most important, however, is the fact that total interest payments are much less on a fifteen-year mortgage than on a thirty-year mortgage. At a 12.5% rate, the interest paid is approximately $45,000 less on the former.

An additional factor that makes shorter-term mortgages a better choice for most consumers is that equity is built much more slowly with long-term mortgages than with short-term mortgages. After paying for fifteen years on a thirty-year mortgage, almost all of the principal is still owed. If the rate were 15%, over $45,000 would still be owed. The average homeowner sells his home after eight years. Table 3 demonstrates the differences in the amounts owed on fifteen- and thirty-year mortgages issued at the same rate. (In fact, fifteen-year loans are generally available for between .25% and .50% less than thirty-year loans.) As can be seen, substantial equity is acquired with a fifteen-year mortgage, whereas almost no equity is built with a thirty-year mortgage.

One advantage of longer mortgages should be noted. Consumers who are in income tax brackets above 30% may find they can make an after-tax profit by taking a longer-term mortgage loan and in-

Table 3
PRINCIPAL OWED ON 15- AND 30-YEAR $50,000 MORTGAGES AFTER 8 YEARS

Interest Rate (%)	*15-Year*	*30-Year*	*$ Difference*
10	$32,365	$46,767	$14,402
11	33,190	47,275	14,085
12	33,994	47,712	13,718
13	34,775	48,086	13,311
14	35,532	48,405	12,873
15	36,365	48,673	12,408
16	36,972	48,901	11,929

vesting the payment difference in tax-exempt municipal bonds. Since mortgage interest is tax deductible, a nominal rate of 13% translates into an effective after-tax loan rate of 9.1% for families in the 30% marginal bracket, and 8.45% for those in the 35% bracket. The yield on tax-exempt municipal bonds is usually 70% of the mortgage loan rate; so, when the mortgage rate is 13%, the yield on municipal bonds will usually be 9.1%. Thus, a family in the 35% marginal tax bracket would be able to borrow at an effective after-tax rate of 8.45%, and invest the funds at a tax-free rate of 9.1%. It should be noted, however, that the tax-exempt market is not free of risk of default.

A final factor to consider in choosing between fifteen-year and thirty-year mortgages is the assumability factor. If the mortgages you are considering are assumable, a longer-term mortgage is more valuable if rates rise. There are two reasons for this. First, the outstanding balance of the mortgage will be higher when the loan is assumed. Second, a lower-than-market-rate assumable mortgage will be in force for a longer period of time.

Adjustable Rate Mortgages (ARMs)

Adjustable rate mortgages became popular in the early 1980s when interest rates on home mortgages began to increase to historically high levels. Lenders, especially S & Ls, found themselves in a serious bind. They had large portfolios of fixed-rate, low-interest mortgages, and had to pay higher savings rates to attract funds as a result of rate deregulation and competition from money market funds. Determined not to get caught in the same vise again, they developed and aggressively marketed ARMs.

ARMs shift the risk of rising interest rates from the lender to the borrower. In its purest form, an ARM is a long-term, self-amortizing loan with a variable interest rate. Interest-rate charges are based on an index over which the lender usually has no control. If the index rate goes up, so does the interest rate charged on the loan, as well as the monthly payments. Conversely, if rates fall, so do the monthly payments and the rate on the loan.

■ Basic Features of All ARMs.

The four basic features of all ARMs are index, margin, initial rate (introductory rate), and adjustment period.

Index.

The index used for ARMs varies with the lending institution. It is almost always a publicly available series of market interest rates beyond the control of the lender. A few lenders, however, use their own cost-of-funds index. The behavior of the index dictates what nappens to the interest rate on the mortgage. All indexes we found in our survey were published monthly by agencies of the U.S. government.

The most common indexes were: one-, three-, and five-year coupon equivalent yields of Treasury securities, the secondary market rate on $100,000 negotiable CDs, the average auction rate of six-month Treasury bills, and the cost of funds to S & Ls, either national or for the Eleventh Federal Home Loan Bank Board (FHLBB) District.

The few lenders who use their own cost of funds as the index for their ARMs have some control over this index. For example, if the lender becomes aggressive in expanding, it may offer very high yields on its CDs, increasing its cost of funds substantially. Further, if the lender becomes less creditworthy as a result of making bad loans, its cost of funds may also increase to a level far higher than the national cost of funds.

In a recent sixteen-city survey, the U.S. League of Savings Institutions (USL) found that the most popular index in use varied from city to city. For example, over 90% of the institutions surveyed in the Atlanta metropolitan area used the one-year U.S. Treasury rate as their index, whereas nearly 60% of those surveyed in Los Angeles used the cost-of-funds index.

Table 4 shows the behavior of the most popular indexes over the past fifteen years. You will notice that the indexes with longer maturities (e.g., the three-year Treasury) generally have higher values than the shorter-term indexes. On the other hand, the shorter-term indexes tend to be more volatile. You will also notice that the $100,000 CD index is substantially higher than the six-month Treasury rate. The national cost-of-funds index has almost always been the lowest, but it has been quite erratic as a result of deregulation.

You should avoid the $100,000 CD index unless it is offered at a low margin. A lender's own cost-of-funds index should always be rejected. Borrowers also may wish to avoid the national cost-of-funds index because of its volatility.

Margin.

The margin is the extra interest lenders add to the index to determine the interest rate on your loan. In our survey, margins ranged from zero to 3.3%, with 2.6% typical.

The margin charged depends on three factors. First is the index used. The lenders charging a 3% margin all use either the six-month or one-year Treasury series as an index, whereas lenders charging no margin used either the 30-year Treasury index or the FHLBB series on mortgages, both of which are substantially higher than other indexes. The differences in the margin tend to make the effective annual interest rates on the loans similar, regardless of the index. The second factor is the optional features of the mortgage. A loan with no interest-rate caps, for example, will carry a lower margin than a loan with caps. Third is the greed of the lender. As in all transactions, some people just charge more.

Table 4
SELECTED INDEXES USED TO SET ARM RATES (ANNUAL AVERAGES)

Year	*1-Year Treasury*	*3-Year Treasury*	*5-Year Treasury*	*Long-Term Fixed-Rate Mortgages*	*S & L Cost of Funds*	*6-Month Treasury Bill Auct.*	*$100,000 CD Security Market*
1970	6.90	7.29	7.38	8.27	5.30	6.56	
1971	4.88	5.65	5.99	7.59	5.38	4.51	
1972	4.96	5.72	5.98	7.45	5.41	4.47	
1973	7.31	6.95	6.87	7.78	5.59	7.18	
1974	8.18	7.82	7.80	8.71	6.14	7.93	
1975	6.76	7.49	7.77	8.75	6.33	6.12	NA
1976	5.88	6.77	7.18	8.76	6.38	5.27	5.62
1977	6.09	6.69	8.32	9.30	6.44	5.51	5.92
1978	8.34	8.29	8.32	9.30	6.67	7.57	8.61
1979	10.67	9.72	9.52	10.48	7.47	10.02	11.44
1980	12.05	11.55	11.48	12.25	8.94	11.37	12.99
1981	14.78	14.44	14.24	14.16	10.92	13.80	15.77
1982	12.27	12.92	13.01	14.47	11.38	11.08	12.57
1983	9.57	10.45	10.80	12.20	9.83	8.75	9.27
1984	10.89	11.89	12.24	11.87	9.85	9.80	10.68
*1985	9.68	10.93	11.43	11.42	9.36	8.92	9.60

* As of March 1985

Initial Rate.

In most cases, the initial rate charged on an ARM is below the index plus margin. In fact, in many cases the interest plus margin was about the same for ARMs as it was for conventional mortgages. The lower initial rate is the carrot being offered to make you accept an ARM rather than a fixed-rate mortgage. Typically, initial rates are about 2.5% below the index plus margin. The initial rate usually remains in effect until the first adjustment period, which is usually one year after the loan is taken.

There are two advantages to a low initial rate. The obvious advantage is that payments during the interval between when you take out the loan and the first adjustment will be lower than they otherwise would have been. This may allow a borrower to qualify for a loan that would otherwise be unobtainable. The USL found that 77% of the institutions it surveyed used the initial rate to determine if a borrower qualified for the ARM he or she was applying for.

The second advantage of a low initial rate applies only when interest-rate caps are a feature of the mortgage contract. Since interest-rate caps generally apply to the initial rate, a lower initial rate limits the maximum rate you might have to pay on your loan.

Beware of "teaser rates." Some mortgages are offered at initial rates that are far below market rates. At the first adjustment, however, they will carry normal market rates, which will result in a very substantial increase in payments. The history of default on such mortgages has been so poor that MGIC, a major mortgage insurer, has refused to insure ARMs with initial rates more than 4% below market rates.

Accepting an ARM with a teaser rate often results in payment shock. To demonstrate, assume you have taken a $50,000, twenty-year ARM at a time when rates on such loans are 12%, but you are given a teaser rate of 7% for the first year. During the first year of the loan, monthly payments will be $387.65. But even if the 12% rate does not change at all, payments in the second year will be $544.43 a month, an increase of nearly $160 a month.

Real estate developers often offer teaser rates to move property in slow housing markets. These developers arrange to "buy down" the interest rate on loans from a particular lender. They pay a fee to the lender in return for being able to offer teaser-rate financing. There are two problems with this sort of arrangement for you as the buyer. First, the developer is likely to capture the cost of the interest-rate "buy-down" by getting a higher price for the house. Second, it is likely that you can find a more attractive loan from another lender, but will be enticed into the loan the developer is offering by the lower teaser rate. If you are considering the purchase of a home that is being offered with a teaser-rate mortgage, you should refuse the mortgage and negotiate a lower price for the home. Then find the best deal available on a mortgage.

If you decide to take a teaser-rate mortgage, be sure you know what it entails. Be sure that you can afford the higher payments after the initial period is over, and that the mortgage is competitive in all other respects.

Adjustment period.

Both the interest rate and monthly loan payments are adjusted at regular intervals on ARMs. The adjustment period is one year at most institutions, six months at many others, and one month at a few. Adjustment intervals of three and five years are widely available, but carry higher interest rates.

The adjustment period for interest rates and the adjustment period for payments sometimes differ. For example, many ARMs adjust interest rates monthly but adjust payments annually. The USL survey found that whereas 80.6% of savings institutions adjusted ARM payments annually, only 40.1% of them adjusted interest rates annually. The rest adjusted rates more frequently. It is preferable to have the adjustment periods for rates and payments coincide.

The advantage of a longer adjustment period is stability in payments. If you are planning to own your house for five years or less, an ARM with a five-year adjustment interval is equivalent to a fixed-rate mortgage and will carry a lower interest rate.

ARMs vs. Conventional Mortgages

Table 5 compares a basic $50,000 thirty-year ARM with a conventional mortgage using actual data for 1979 to 1985. The features of the ARM used are typical, based on our survey: The index is the one-year Treasury security, the margin is 1.5%, and the initial rate is 9%. The fixed rate is 10.48%.

Table 5
BASIC ARM VS. FIXED-RATE MORTGAGE, 1979–1985

Year	***Monthly Payments*** *ARM*	***Monthly Payments*** *Fixed-Rate*
1979	$402.31	$456.62
1980	519.11	456.62
1981	571.64	456.62
1982	677.35	456.62
1983	580.89	456.62
1984	482.45	456.62
1985	529.08	456.62
Total payments	$45,154	$38,356
Total interest paid	43,388	35,397
Balance owed	48,234	47,541

As can be seen, a person taking a typical uncapped ARM in January 1979 would have fared much worse than someone taking a conventional mortgage. Over the seven years of the loan, the former would have made almost $7000 more in payments and would still owe $700 more after seven years than the homeowner who took a conventional mortgage at a higher initial rate. This, of course, would not have been the case if the ARM had been taken in 1981 or 1982, since rates have come down considerably since that time.

As a general rule, ARMs make some sense when mortgage rates are very high, but not when they are moderate or low. Of course, knowing how high is very high over the long term is virtually impossible. In the middle 1970s, a 9% interest rate on mortgages was considered to be outrageous, and, in fact, violated usury laws in some states. No economist would forecast rates over the coming fifteen or thirty years.

Optional Features of ARMs

■ Interest Rate Caps.

Interest-rate caps are an essential feature of ARMs. Except under the most unusual circumstances, consumers should not take an ARM without them. Interest-rate caps can be viewed as an insurance policy against rising rates. If ARMs transfer interest-rate risk from lenders to borrowers, caps limit that risk. The range between the initial mortgage rate and the maximum rate can be viewed as the deductible on an insurance policy. The lower the deductible, the greater the risk to the underwriter, and the higher the premium. So, too, with rate caps. The lower the caps, the higher the cost in terms of the margin over the index.

All but one lender in our survey offered capped loans. In fact, interest-capped loans with a 2% per-year maximum adjustment and a 5% life-of-the-loan maximum adjustment have become standard in the industry. The typical margin for such a loan is 2.6%. According to the USL survey, more than 70% of ARMs given had annual interest-rate caps, and 93.5% of ARMs had lifetime caps on interest rates.

Table 6 demonstrates the advantage of an ARM with interest-rate

Table 6
UNCAPPED vs. CAPPED ARMs

Year	***Payments*** *Uncapped ARM*	***Payments*** *Capped ARM*
1979	$402.31	$402.31
1980	519.11	475.05
1981	571.64	549.98
1982	677.35	587.96
1983	580.89	587.96
1984	492.45	520.58
1985	529.08	568.20
Total payment	$45,154	$44,304
Total interest	43,388	42,538
Balance owed	48,234	48,234

caps over one that has no caps. It compares the ARM in Table 5, which was a $50,000 thirty-year mortgage with an initial rate of 9%, a margin of 1.5%, and used the six-month Treasury bill series as an index, to a capped ARM for the same amount and term. This capped ARM limits interest-rate adjustments to 2% a year, and to 5% for the life of the loan. It also uses the six-month Treasury bill series, but has a margin of 2.6%.

As can be seen, interest-rate caps worked out well for the home buyer. Monthly payments were lower for the capped mortgage in 1980, 1981, and 1982. Total payments and interest paid over the seven years were $850 less. It should be noted, however, that there is no guarantee that this will always happen. If the mortgage had been taken out in 1982, for example, the uncapped mortgage would have been preferable.

The most significant advantage of the capped mortgage is that the maximum payment is defined, whereas there is no maximum for uncapped mortgages. In the example, the home buyer would have had monthly payments of $677.35 with the uncapped mortgage in 1982, whereas the maximum at any point for the capped mortgage was $587.96.

When obtaining a capped loan, be sure you know what rate the cap applies to. While most caps apply to the initial interest rate, this is often not the case when the mortgage is issued with a teaser rate, and never the case when the initial rate is lowered by a seller buy-down. For example, in August 1985, Green Point Savings Bank in Brooklyn offered an ARM at an initial rate of 9%. Its ad announced that the mortgage had 2% per-year and 3% lifetime interest-rate caps. In much smaller print, the reader learned that the caps applied to the value of the index plus margin at the time the loan was issued, which was then 13%.

Three- and five-year caps are also available. Under such a plan, the interest rate and payments are fixed for three or five years, and then are adjusted annually, subject to some maximum. This would be the ideal mortgage if you do not plan to own your home for more than six or seven years. It can be shown that in even a worst-case scenario, such a mortgage is preferable to a fixed-rate mortgage for the short-term homeowner.

■ Payment Caps and Negative Amortization.

Many lenders offer ARMs with caps on the yearly increase in payments. The payment cap is often combined with interest-rate caps, but is sometimes the only cap offered. According to the USL survey, 3.2% of the ARMs given had only payment caps. Payment caps do not prevent the interest rate on your loan from going up. If the interest rate rises to the point where your mortgage payments are not large enough to pay all of the interest you are liable for, the difference between the interest charged and your payments is added to the principal of your loan. This is called "negative amortization," because, rather than making progress toward paying off your loan, you are adding to it.

Negative amortization is not permitted to go on forever. Most lenders recompute payments every five years to make certain that the loan is fully amortized over its initial term. Further, if the principal of the loan ever reaches 125% of its initial value, most lenders will increase payments to assure that the loan is paid off over its term. If negative amortization occurs during the last five years of the loan's life, a balloon payment will be due.

Since the lender's exposure to interest-rate risk is not increased by agreeing to payment caps, this option can be obtained without additional cost in most cases. Even though this cap is free, it may not be very suitable for most buyers, since payments can suddenly increase by huge amounts.

Table 7 compares, using historical data, an ARM with rate caps of 2% per year and 5% for the life of the loan to an ARM that has only a 7.5% annual-payment cap. Both ARMs are for $50,000, have initial rates of 9%, and have terms of thirty years. They both use the six-month Treasury bill index. The ARM with rate caps has a margin of 2.6%; the one with only payment caps has a margin of 1.5%.

Table 7 demonstrates why loans that have only payment caps should be avoided. Whereas payments were lower in every year but 1983 for this ARM, interest charged on the loan was over $4000 more. Further, at the end of seven years the home buyer with this

Table 7
ARM with Interest-Rate Caps vs. ARM with Payment Cap Only

Year	**Payments** *Rate-Capped ARM*	**Payments** *Payment-Capped ARM*
1979	$402.31	$402.31
1980	475.05	432.48
1981	549.98	464.92
1982	587.96	499.79
1983	587.96	537.27
1984	520.58	548.71
1985	568.20	589.86
Total payments	$ 45,154	$ 41,704
Total interest	42,538	46,736
Balance owed	48,234	55,032

loan owed more than $5000 more than when the loan was first taken.

The example does not show the most serious disadvantage of ARMs with only payment caps—a sudden and unexpected jump in monthly payments in adjustment years. Assume that interest rates rose in 1983 and that as a consequence the rate for 1984 was 16.28%, the same as it was in 1982. Since 1984 marked the fifth anniversary of the loan, payments would be adjusted to pay off the loan in the remaining twenty-five years of its life. The monthly payments would increase to $769.12, a jump of over $230 per month. If the homeowner could not meet these payments, he or she could be forced to sell the home. The combination of the negative amortization and real estate commissions coupled with a distress sale are likely to wipe out all of the homeowner's equity. This is not a worst-case scenario. The homeowner's loss would have been even greater if the calculation had begun with 1978 instead of 1979.

The worst-case scenario would have interest rates escalate to a very high level immediately, and remain high. If this should happen, the maximum of 125% of the initial loan amount could be reached very quickly. It is possible that after five years the home buyer would owe $62,500 on his $50,000 loan. If the rate was 16.28%, payments would increase from $537.27 to $863.06. It is not unlikely that such a homeowner would be forced into bankruptcy.

Payment caps are seldom provided alone; most often, they are combined with interest-rate caps. Even when this is the case, however, it is not clear that it is a good idea to choose this option. Table 8 compares the interest-rate-capped ARM of the earlier example to one that has a 7.5% per-year payment cap in addition to the interest-rate caps.

This table shows both the advantages and disadvantages of combining payment caps with interest-rate caps. The advantage in this example was that payments increased gradually over the course of seven years. As things worked out, they never increased by more than 7.5% a year, even at the five-year adjustment period. The disadvantage of the arrangement was that not only did the home buyer fail to build equity during those seven years, but he or she actually ended up owing almost $2500 more than when the loan began. Whereas total payments were almost $2200 less with payment caps, interest charged was almost $2100 more. Note also that the worst-

Table 8
INTEREST-RATE-CAPPED ARMs WITHOUT AND WITH PAYMENT CAPS

Year	***Payments*** *Without Payment Cap*	***Payment*** *With Payment Cap*
1979	$402.31	$402.31
1980	475.05	432.48
1981	549.98	464.92
1982	587.96	499.79
1983	587.96	537.27
1984	520.58	565.18
1985	568.20	607.57
Total payments	$ 44,304	$ 42,114
Interest	42,538	44,599
Balance owed	48,234	52,485

case scenario described above for only payment caps is also possible with loans that have both payment and interest-rate caps.

■ Convertability.

Some lenders allow an ARM to be converted to a conventional mortgage at the option of the borrower. Under this feature, the borrower must agree to pay the then current rate on fixed mortgages, which recently has been as high or higher than the rate being charged on existing ARMs. In addition, lenders generally charge a fee of 1% of the mortgage principal. Lenders offering a convertability feature usually limit it to the first five years of the mortgage.

Convertability is a desirable feature in an ARM, but not one you should pay much for, since you can always refinance your mortgage for a loan origination fee of two or three points, provided it does not include a prepayment fee. Further, if you decide that it is wise to shift from an ARM to a fixed-rate mortgage, converting at the same institution prevents you from seeking lower rates elsewhere. Remember, a savings of two points on loan origination fees is worth only between ¼% and ½% on the rate. We found much wider variations than that in the rates being offered in any given city.

Other Types of Mortgages

■ Graduated-Payment Mortgage.

Graduated-payment mortgages (GPMs) can have either a fixed or a variable rate, and are designed for home buyers who expect to experience substantial increases in their incomes over the course of several years. In the early years of a GPM, the scheduled payments are less than what would be required to fully amortize the loan, and negative amortization occurs. After five or ten years, depending on the terms of the loan, payments are increased to pay off the entire loan in the number of years remaining. For example, assume that you wish to borrow $50,000 for thirty years at a fixed rate of

14%. Your monthly payments would be $592.44 with a conventional mortgage. If, instead, you choose a GPM, with monthly payments of $500 for the first five years, your payments would increase to $638.35 a month after five years, and the outstanding balance on the mortgage would be over $57,000.

The danger of a GPM is that you may be unable to meet the higher payments when they come due in five or ten years. You would then be forced to refinance, incurring loan origination fees, and possibly prepayment penalties as well. It is possible that you could lose your home as a result. Further, the combination of accumulated negative amortization, real estate commissions, and a lower price due to a forced sale could easily wipe out all your equity in the home. GPMs are extremely dangerous loans. The default rate on these mortgages is currently over five times as high as on conventional mortgages.

Combining a GPM with an ARM greatly increases the risk of higher payments. Some GPMs, however, increase payments every year by a fixed percentage, generally 7.5%. This feature would lessen the extent to which a borrower would be subject to negative amortization.

■ Balloon-Payment Mortgages and Seller Financing.

Balloon-payment mortgages are issued at fixed rates, and have payments based on long amortization periods, but must be paid off well before they are fully amortized. A typical example would be a mortgage that has monthly payments that would amortize the loan over thirty years, but that must be paid back in full at the end of five years. At that point, the borrower will still owe almost the entire initial principal of the mortgage and will either have to refinance the loan or pay it back in a single balloon payment. Balloon-payment mortgages are common when sellers finance the purchase of a home.

For example, assume you wish to buy a house for $100,000 and can make a $20,000 down payment. The seller has a 9% assumable mortgage worth $10,000, with five years left on it. If you assume the first mortgage, your monthly payments will be $207.58. The seller then finances the remaining $70,000 with an 11% second mortgage with monthly payments calculated as if the balance were to be amortized over thirty years, and requires a balloon payment at the end of five years. The monthly payments on the second mortgage will be $666.63, so that your total monthly mortgage payments will be $874.21. The balloon payment, due in five years, will be about $68,000.

The attraction of this type of mortgage package is that you are able to obtain financing at below market rates. The financing package presented above would, typically, be written when mortgage rates were around 13%. If this were the case, a thirty-year mortgage at market rates would have monthly payments of $884.96. Another advantage of this arrangement over a conventional mortgage at market rates is that equity is built much more quickly. The home buyer builds $12,000 in equity with the financing package described above, whereas with a conventional mortgage at market rates he or she would have acquired only about $1,500 in equity. The difference in equity is a consequence of the favorable interest rates on both loans.

There are several problems with this sort of financing, however. First, you may be forced to pay a much higher interest rate when the balloon payment comes due. Second, you may not be able to secure financing at any price in five years. To protect against this, be sure there is an escape clause in the mortgage document that requires the mortgage holder to extend the mortgage on a year-to-year basis if financing is unavailable at the time your balloon payment is due. Third, you lose many legal protections when you engage in seller financing. It is most important that you have an attorney examine and approve the mortgage document.

Balloon-payment mortgages are also sometimes issued by lending institutions. These are a variation of ARMs, but offer none of the protections given by rate caps. The typical balloon-payment mortgage issued by a lending institution guarantees refinancing at market rates when the balloon payment is due. If the home buyer in the previous example took an $80,000 mortgage with a five-year balloon, he would have to refinance almost $78,500 at the end of five years. If rates had risen to 17%, monthly payments would be $1,128.67, an increase of $243. There are no advantages to this sort of financing, and it should be avoided.

■ Growing Equity Mortgages.

A recent innovation in the mortgage market, growing equity mortgages (GEMs), combines fixed interest rates with increasing monthly payments. With such a mortgage, a borrower can pay off a thirty-year mortgage in fifteen years or less. These mortgages are recommended only if you are confident you will experience above-average increases in income over time.

The increases in monthly payments are based on an agreed-upon index, often the Department of Commerce's index of after-tax per-capita income. Since all of the increased payments are applied to the principal of the mortgage, the mortgage will be paid back much faster than with straight amortization. In fact, GEMs are the exact opposite of negative amortization.

The advantage of a GEM is that you receive the benefit of lower monthly payments during the early years of the mortgage, because payments are calculated as if the mortgage were to be amortized over thirty years, whereas payments in fact increase gradually with the general increase in per-capita income. Of course, if your income increases much more slowly than the national average, you may be unable to afford the increased payments. If this was the case, you would be forced to refinance, incurring loan origination fees and possibly prepayment penalties as well. If interest rates had risen substantially, you could have to sell your home.

■ FHA Mortgages.

Congress created the Federal Housing Administration (FHA) in 1934 to insure mortgage loans made to low- and moderate-income families. The loans are made by conventional lenders who agree to write FHA insured loans.

FHA loans are issued with down payments of as little as 3% on the first $25,000, and 5% on the remainder. For a single family residence, the mortgage insurance premium is 3.8% of the loan amount. Thus, on a $50,000 FHA loan, the mortgage insurance premium would be $1,900.

In addition to requiring very low down payments, FHA loans offer several other advantages. First, the interest rate charged is often from one to one-half percentage points lower than that charged on conventional loans. Second, FHA loans are fully assumable. Finally, no points are paid by the buyer on FHA loans.

There are several disadvantages to FHA loans that may make them unobtainable for most home buyers. First, they require maximum mortgage amounts, which vary from area to area. Second, if you buy a home using this financing, you will be unable to obtain a second mortgage. Third, since FHA loans carry below-market rates, many lenders will not make them. Those that do often require the seller to pay points to make up for the lower rate. The seller may not be willing to do this.

■ VA Mortgages.

The Veterans Administration (VA) guarantees the mortgage loans of veterans and servicemen, subject to certain criteria. The VA will guarantee up to $27,500 of a mortgage, and charge no insurance premium for this. The amount of this guarantee is increased periodically.

VA loans generally require no down payment. However, lenders may require some down payment on a portion of the loan not guaranteed by the VA. Lenders may also require private mortgage insurance for the unguaranteed portion of the loan.

The VA requires that all homes financed using its guarantees be appraised. The VA will not issue guarantees for more than the reasonable value of the property. If the property desired is priced above its reasonable value, the veteran can have the sale voided, or purchase the property, with the VA only guaranteeing the loan for the reasonable value of the property.

Shopping for a Mortgage

It pays to spend a great deal of time and effort to make certain you are getting the best possible mortgage. You should be prepared to spend as much as several days, full time, in finding the right one.

Most major metropolitan newspapers run listings of the mortgage terms available from different lenders. These lists lack detail, but they are a reasonable starting point. In addition, most real estate agents have more detailed information on available sources of mortgage money. Finally, private firms in a number of cities make their living by surveying the regional mortgage markets. Their research is generally available for a fee of about $20.

Once you have obtained the published information, you should call the most favorable institutions and extract as much information about terms and details as you can by phone. The worksheets at the end of this chapter should be helpful for this purpose. In addition to the traditional mortgage lenders, banks and S & Ls, you should also check out your credit union and insurance companies

When you have finally decided to make a formal application, it is smart to try to negotiate a better deal from the lender. Nothing is written in stone, and you have nothing to lose by trying.

When to Refinance a Mortgage

If you took out a mortgage when interest rates were higher than they now are, you may wish to consider refinancing at the current lower rate. Since there are costs to refinancing, timing is important in making the decision. If you refinance today, and rates continue to fall, you will incur substantial additional costs if you decide to refinance a second time. On the other hand, if rates rise, the opportunity to refinance profitably will be lost.

There are no basic formulas for predicting when rates will bottom out. However, you can consider several factors when deciding to refinance.

First, evaluate all the costs involved. These will include closing costs on the new loan, and possibly a prepayment penalty. Second, evaluate your savings over the next two to three years. If your savings exceed the costs, and if you plan to own your own home for more than the pay-back period, you probably should refinance. As a general rule of thumb, interest rates will have to have fallen by one to two points for refinancing to meet the above test.

If you decide to refinance, it is a good idea to talk to your mortgage holder after you have discussed a new loan with another lender. You may be able to use the lower rate offered by the other lender as a bargaining chip. Your original lender may waive some or all of the loan origination fees.

A complication in determining if refinancing a mortgage is financially sound is the time value of money. This is especially important if you plan to own your home for a number of years. Table 9 gives the minimum reduction in monthly payments necessary per $1000 in refinancing costs to make refinancing worthwhile.

To demonstrate Table 9, suppose you plan on owning your home for five more years, and are considering refinancing. If your total refinancing costs are $5000 (closing costs, legal fees, prepayment penalties, etc.), you would need to realize a reduction in mortgage payments of $110 per month ($22 × 5) to make refinancing worthwhile when interest rates are 10%. If you intend to own your home for fifteen more years, however, a monthly reduction in mortage payments of $55 per month ($11 × 5) would make refinancing worthwhile.

Note that Table 9 does not take into account tax considerations. Not all refinancing fees are deductible, while interest payments are. On the other hand, most refinancing costs are immediately deductible as interest, while the tax savings from the higher interest payments on your existing mortgage are spread out over many years. In general, tax considerations will often result in a wash, so the above table is still a reasonable guide.

Refinancing over the same period will lower monthly payments. But you should consider leaving your payments at the same level, and taking a shorter-term mortgage. The savings in interest will be much greater than if you merely take a new loan at a lower rate.

Table 9
IS REFINANCING WORTHWHILE? **Minimum Required Reduction in Monthly Payments per $1000 in Refinancing Costs**

New Interest	*Years You Plan on Owning Home*							
Rate (%)	*1 yr.*	*2 yrs.*	*3 yrs.*	*4 yrs.*	*5 yrs.*	*7 yrs.*	*10 yrs.*	*15 yrs.*
8	$87	$46	$32	$25	$21	$16	$13	$10
9	88	46	32	25	21	17	13	11
10	88	47	33	26	22	17	14	11
11	89	47	33	26	22	18	14	12
12	89	48	34	27	23	18	15	12
13	90	48	34	27	23	19	15	13
14	90	49	35	28	24	19	16	14

W O R K S H E E T 1

Use this worksheet when shopping for a conventional mortgage.

Application fee __________

Appraisal & credit
check fees __________

Loan origination
fees
Points __________
Other __________

Interest rate __________

APR __________

Monthly payments __________

Escrow required? __________

Interest paid on escrow? __________

Minimum down payment
Without PMI __________
With PMI __________

Cost of PMI __________

Assumability __________

Prepayment penalty __________

Late payment fee __________

Note: Data should be gathered for both long and short-term loans.

W O R K S H E E T 2

Use this worksheet when stopping for an ARM. Refer to worksheet 1 to gather information on common fees, penalties, escrow, etc.

Fixed-rate APR ____________

Initial rate ____________

Index ____________

Name ____________

Current rate ____________

Margin ____________

Adjustment period

Rate ____________

Payments ____________

Initial payment ____________

Time initial payment lasts ____________

Interest-rate caps

Interval ____________

Per interval ____________

Lifetime ____________

Payment caps

Percent per year ____________

Payment adjustment period ____________

Negative amortization

Maximum ____________

What is done if maximum is reached? ____________

Convertability

When ____________

Cost ____________

Questions to Ask about Monthly Payment Amounts

What will happen to monthly payments in twelve months if the index rate

- Stays the same? __________
- Goes up 2%? __________
- Goes up 5%? __________
- Goes down 2%? __________

What will happen to monthly payments after three years if the index rate

- Stays the same? __________
- Goes up 2% per year? __________
- Goes up 3% per year? __________
- Goes down 2% per year? __________
- Goes down 3% per year? __________

$ ¢ $ ¢ $

¢ $ ¢ $ ¢

$ ¢ $ ¢ $

¢ $ ¢ $ ¢

11

How to Resolve Banking Complaints

How to Complain

If a banking institution has treated you unfairly, pursue your grievance. Do not worry about whether your complaint can be justified legally. How long it takes you to resolve your complaint often depends on how you complain. We recommend the following approach.

Identify both your problem and the remedy you seek. It may surprise you to learn that many consumers who complain have not thought seriously about the latter. They are just "mad as hell and not going to take it any more." But you need a solution to the problem that the banking institution can act on.

Explain your problem and remedy to several friends. This will help ensure that you understand and can describe both. Also, ask them if the remedy sounds justified in light of the grievance. Generally, it is counterproductive to ask the banking institution not only to resolve the specific problem, but also to compensate you generously for inconvenience and aggravation.

Describe the complaint in writing as clearly and concisely as you can. Document any controversial aspects of the problem. For example, keep a record of any phone conversations with bank employees, including dates and names. If a monthly bill is in dispute, make a photocopy of the statement.

Whenever possible, complaint letters should be typed. They should include the following information:

- Type of service
- Date and location of purchase or transaction
- Brief statement of problem
- History of problem and your attempts to resolve it
- Resolution you desire
- Request for action in a specific period of time
- Your address
- Your work and home phone numbers

Enclose copies of relevant documents and keep a copy of the letter for your records.

Where to Complain

You can complain to the following agencies, in the order listed:

- The bank or S & L
- Federal Reserve Board
- State or local complaint agency
- State banking department
- Small claims court or attorney
- Begin with the offending institution. Go directly to the unit with which you dealt. If it was a bank branch, talk to the manager. If it was the credit card department, contact its director. Do not be afraid to make a personal appearance, particularly at a branch. But calling first may save you time. When you call,

first find out the name of the bank official to whom you wish to speak. Then ask to speak to him or her.

In verbal communications with bank employees, speak calmly but firmly. Above all, *be persistent*. Do not let them pass the buck or ignore you. If they speak rudely, ask for their names and report them to their boss, or boss's boss.

If contacting a branch or department does not speedily resolve your problem, go immediately to the top. Write a letter to the president of the institution and, a week after it is sent, call his or her office to ask what action has been taken. In virtually all cases, the president will refer the complaint back to the first unit you contacted. But you can be assured that it will now receive special attention. If it is not resolved to your satisfaction, call the president's office again, to inform him or her you still have a problem.

If you are still dissatisfied, write to the Office of Consumer and Community Affairs of the Federal Reserve Board. In most cases, they will handle your complaint or refer it to the most appropriate government agency. Their address is:

Board of Governors of the Federal Reserve System
Office of Consumer and Community Affairs
20th and C Street, NW
Washington, DC 20551

You can call them at (202) 452-3946.

This office handles only complaints against state-chartered members of the Federal Reserve System—about 1000 institutions. But they will refer grievances against other banking institutions to an appropriate federal agency, such as the Comptroller of the Currency, the Federal Deposit Insurance Corporation, the Federal Savings and Loan Insurance Corporation, the National Credit Union Administration, or the Federal Trade Commission, or in certain situations, to a state agency. Most banking institutions are regulated by the federal government, but the relatively small number of state-chartered institutions uninsured by a federal agency are not.

If you are still dissatisfied, contact a state or local complaint agency. Different regions are served by different agencies. Most contain at least one of the following:

- A state government protection agency, usually part of the Attorney General's office, but sometimes part of another department, such as Commerce
- Local government protection agencies run by large cities or counties
- Call-for-Action offices, which are affiliated with a local television or radio station
- A newspaper action line column
- A nonprofit consumer group that handles complaints

These agencies are often listed in the yellow pages of your local phone directory under "Consumer Groups." City Hall, a local consumer reporter or an all-purpose hot line may be able to refer you to the appropriate agency.

There are two other organizations you may consider if all other agencies fail. One is the local office of the Better Business Bureau BBB offices keep excellent records of complaints brought to their attention by consumers. But they do not see themselves primarily as complaint-resolution agencies. Generally, their complaint handling will consist of sending a letter to the bank (or other merchant) informing it of your complaint.

The second agency is the banking department in your state, which is called by different names in different states. Call your state government information line for the name and number of this department. But do not expect quick action or satisfaction. Traditionally, these offices have been more sympathetic to banks than to consumers. And most are understaffed.

The last resort for consumers with unresolved complaints is an attorney or small claims court. Most banking grievances involve too little money to be of much interest to an attorney. Yet there are exceptions, such as complaints that involve Truth-in-Lending violations. For most complainants, small claims courts are more useful. These local courts settle a variety of small claims. You can represent yourself—you do not need an attorney. And the cost of filing is minimal, usually under $15. When you visit the court to file your grievance, ask if your complaint is appropriate to be heard by a small claims judge.

Always keep in mind that, at the very least, a bank or an S & L owes a serious response to customers with complaints. This response is an obligation of all sellers that simply goes with the territory. To the extent consumers complain responsibly about problems, most banks and other sellers will recognize this obligation.

About the Authors

DR. NAPHTALI HOFFMAN serves as Associate Professor of Economics at Elmira College in Elmira, New York. He is co-author of *The Cleveland BankBook.*

DR. STEPHEN BROBECK serves as Executive Director of the Consumer Federation of America, the nation's largest consumer advocacy organization. He is co-author of *The Cleveland BankBook* and *The Product Safety Book,* and author of numerous other consumer publications. Brobeck is frequently asked by Congress and by national press to comment on consumer banking issues.

JACK GILLIS serves as Director of Public Affairs for the Consumer Federation of America. He is author of *The Car Book,* co-author of *The Child Safety Book,* editor of *The Product Safety Book,* and writes a regular monthly consumer column for *Good Housekeeping.*

Index

D

E

F

G

H

I

J

K

L

M

N

O

P

R

S

T

U

V

W

Y

Z